W9-AQE-724

Octavio Paz

Twayne's World Authors Series
Latin American Literature

David Foster, Editor
Arizona State University

TWAS 783

OCTAVIO PAZ
(1914–   )
Photograph by Rafael Doniz

Octavio Paz

By Jason Wilson

King's College, London

Twayne Publishers
A Division of G.K. Hall & Co. • Boston

For Tomasina, Lucinda, and Camila

Octavio Paz

Jason Wilson

Copyright © 1986 by G.K. Hall & Co.
All Rights Reserved
Published by Twayne Publishers
A Division of G.K. Hall & Co.
70 Lincoln Street
Boston, Massachusetts 02111

Copyedited under the supervision of Lewis DeSimone
Book production by Marne B. Sultz
Book design by Barbara Anderson

Typeset in 11 pt. Garamond
by Modern Graphics, Inc., Weymouth, Massachusetts

Printed on permanent/durable acid-free paper
and bound in the United States of America

Library of Congress Cataloging in Publication Data

Wilson, Jason, 1944–
  Octavio Paz.

  (Twayne's world authors series ; TWAS 783. Latin American literature)
  Bibliography: p. 155
  Includes index.
  1. Paz, Octavio, 1914–   —Criticism and
interpretation.   I. Title.   II. Series: Twayne's world authors series ; TWAS
783.   III. Series: Twayne's world authors series. Latin American literature.
PQ7297.P285Z97   1986   861   86–9998
ISBN 0–8057–6630–8

Contents

About the Author

Jason Wilson was born in Mauritius in 1944 and educated in Britain. He received his B.A. (Hons) in Spanish at King's College, University of London (1966). He was graduate assistant at Brown University (1967–68), then research fellow at Liverpool University's Center for Latin American Studies (1968–69) and lecturer in Latin American literature at King's College and the Institute of Latin American Studies, University of London (1969–81). He is visiting lecturer at King's College (1981–). He has researched in Mexico (1966) and Argentina (1970, 1974, 1976, 1980).

He has published *Octavio Paz: A Study of his Poetics* (1979; Spanish translation, 1980), articles on Paz, Vallejo, Felisberto Hernández, Cortázar, Artaud, W. H. Hudson, Von Humboldt, and Charles Darwin, and many reviews. He is married and has three daughters.

Preface

Octavio Paz is Latin America's best-known living poet. He has accompanied his vivid poetry with remarkably lucid essays, ranging from critiques of Lévi-Strauss to appreciations of André Breton, Jorge Guillén, Rubén Darío, and Henri Michaux, among many others, and culminating in a masterful study of Sor Juana (1982). This book identifies the cohesive thread running through this brilliant output of poems and essays in terms of a clash between what Paz has called history and poetry. We take a chronological look and explore the poetry, which begins with early enthusiastic support for revolutionary change in society, proceeds to a disenchantment with this social revolution, and terminates in discovery of an alternative way of changing man through art associated with Paz's close links with the surrealists. This leads to the crucial idea that the real revolution is mental—concerned with our inner space—a view resulting from Paz's years in India. Within Paz's work there are several confrontations with the political realities, art, and nationalistic mentality of Mexico. Ultimately, we glance at Paz's democratic stance against all authoritarian states where poetry becomes a purge of the language of power. Paz's work is a constant combat with his times, and we point this out not biographically but as it takes place within his work itself—in the way that Paz described Luis Cernuda's poetry as a spiritual biography. This study follows Paz's changes and views his multifaceted work as a continuous disquisition on how to be free in a repressive world, where brief moments of freedom may be experienced in the poems as acts of consciousness. In this sense, Paz's work transcends the barriers of culture and language to become a truly universal art.

The difficulty facing any exegesis of Paz's work is exactly that quality that has given it such prestige and respect: namely, an enthusiastic, passionate, and probing style displaying an acute illuminating degree of self-consciousness. In order not to repeat less elegantly what Paz has already written and to make sense of a bewilderingly diverse output, this study locates an ever-renewing center in Paz's moral stance; a drive to free the mind expressed through art and affirming a set of values against whatever impoverishes man's potential.

I would especially like to thank Octavio Paz for allowing me to quote from his works. Unless otherwise noted I have cited from his *Poemas (1935–1975)* published in 1979, abbreviating it to *P* with page number in the text. The poetry is set first in Spanish followed by my translation. References to secondary sources have been kept to a minimum, and I have noted the most useful in the notes and bibliography.

Jason Wilson

King's College, London

Chronology

1914   Octavio Paz born on 31 March in Mexico City. Brought up in Mixcoac where he attends primary school.

1927–1929   Secondary school in Mexico City.

1931   Publishes first poem. Founds *Barandal*, first literary review.

1933   *Luna silvestre*, first book of poems.

1936   Visits and works in Yucatan.

1937   Marries Elena Garro.

1937–1938   Visits Republican Spain to attend the Writer's Congress. Meets Neruda, Vallejo, Buñuel, and Miguel Hernández. *Raíz del hombre*.

1938   In Paris. Meets Robert Desnos. In Mexico founds *Taller* (1938–41), a literary review.

1942   *A la orilla del mundo.*

1943   Helps found and edit *El hijo pródigo* (1943–45), a literary review.

1943–1945   In the United States on a Guggenheim.

1945–1951   In Paris; from 1946 as Mexican cultural attaché. Befriends André Breton and his surrealist group.

1949   *Libertad bajo palabra.*

1950   *El laberinto de la soledad* (second revised edition in 1959).

1951   *¿Aguila o sol?*

1952   Visits India and Japan.

1954   *Semillas para un himno.*

1956   *El arco y la lira. La hija de Rappaccini* (play) performed.

1957   *Piedra de sol.*

1958   *La estación violenta.*

1959–1962 Lives in Paris.

1960 *Libertad bajo palabra* (revised edition in 1968).

1962 *Salamandra.*

1962–1968 Mexican ambassador in India.

1963 International Poetry Prize, Brussels.

1964 Marries Marie-José Tramini.

1967 *Blanco.* Enters Colegio Nacional, Mexico.

1968 Resigns his post in protest at the massacre of students just before Mexico hosted the Olympic Games.

1969 *Ladera este; Conjunciones y disyunciones.*

1970 *Posdata.* Simón Bolívar chair at Cambridge University.

1971–1976 Founds *Plural,* literary review.

1971–1972 Charles Eliot Norton Professor at Harvard.

1972 *Renga.*

1974 *Los hijos del limo,* his Harvard lectures.

1975 *Pasado en claro.*

1976 Founds *Vuelta,* literary review.

1977 Jerusalem Prize.

1979 *Poemas (1935–75).* Golden Eagle Prize, Nice.

1980 Olin Yoliztli Prize, Mexico. Honorary degree, Harvard.

1981 Cervantes Prize, Madrid.

1982 *Sor Juana Inés de la Cruz o las trampas de la fe.* Neustadt Prize, University of Oklahoma.

1984 Peace Prize, Frankfurt.

Chapter One
The Early Years: Spain, Politics, and Poetry

Octavio Paz was born in 1914 in Mexico City in the middle of a bloody and chaotic revolution. However, he avoided this gruesome turmoil and was brought up in a large rundown house in Mixcoac by his pious mother—Josefina Lozano, daughter of Spanish immigrants—a spinster aunt (who introduced him to authors like Victor Hugo and Rousseau), and his paternal grandfather. His father, Octavio Paz, a journalist and lawyer who defended the peasant revolutionary Emiliano Zapata (1877?–1919) in New York and who helped introduce agrarian reform after the Revolution, was usually absent. Paz evoked this family in his long poem *Pasado en claro* (The past clarified/copied out, 1915). His grandfather was influential: he had fought against the French (1862–68) and supported the dictator Porfirio Díaz (1830–1915); he had written novels and possessed a good library vital to Paz's early literary preparation. The library was rich in classical authors, Spanish classics, and Mexican *modernistas* like Amado Nervo (1870–1919), but stopped at about 1900.[1]

Protected by his religious mother and educated by French Marist fathers, Paz was immune from the violence and political maneuverings of those revolutionary days. Yet he grew up in a Mexico coming to terms with its unique Revolution, a period (1917–) often analyzed by Paz but never as a personal experience.

Paz's passion for the fate and history of his country forms part of an intellectual awakening to the dilemmas of postrevolutionary Mexico's possible directions: the Ateneo group, especially José Vasconcelos (1881–1951) and Alfonso Reyes (1889–1959), the philosopher Samuel Ramos (1897–1959), the muralist painters, novelists, anthropologists, and archeologists combined to form a tradition, to which Paz himself actively contributed, that sought to rediscover Mexico's identity. But this nationalistic soul-searching did not determine Paz's early classical and conservative literary development. Only as an adolescent in the 1920s did he discover his own voice

1

through the dissident poets congregated round the magazine *Contemporáneos* (1928–31) whose European cultural curiosity led Paz to discover the modern Spanish poets in Gerardo Diego's *Antología* (1932) and then back in time to Juan Ramón Jiménez (1881–1958) and Antonio Machado (1875–1939). This discovery of a non-Mexican modern tradition forms part of our study.[2]

Paz came of age as a young poet in the crisis years that marked the 1929 Wall Street crash, the rise of fascism, and the appeal of Russian socialism—but from the perspective of a Mexico puzzled by the violence and changes in a seemingly unique revolution that had closed the nation to experiences other than its own. The quality and temper of Paz's writings must be seen in the light of his need to make an idealistic order out of his times's confusions and who as a religiously educated but agnostic young poet turned elsewhere for models in a climate hostile to anything that was not zenophobically Mexican.

The Moral Stance

As early as 1939, on his return from fallen Republican Spain, Paz wrote concerning Emilio Prados (1899–1962)—in Paz's literary review *Taller*—that "poetry, the best poetry, is a conduct: it expresses itself in acts. It is an image come to life."[3] Far more urgent than writing a good poem, an aesthetic ivory tower response to the twentieth-century experience of competing ideologies, this suggests an urge to act out the values of poetry as a way of changing man. The images released by the poet on paper change the poet and make this change in consciousness the real poem. By 1939 Paz had discovered his identity as a poet, not as a Mexican nor a revolutionary. What unites artists as diverse as Tamayo, Cernuda, Breton, Michaux, and Villaurrutia is their moral stance toward art. Paz rescued this moral vision from the collapse of surrealism: "Surrealism is not a poetry but a poetic and even more decisively, a vision of the world."[4] In 1954 Paz stated that surrealism seduced him beyond its theories about automatic writing because of its "intransigent affirmation of certain values."[5] Paz expanded this notion to include his own work. To Claude Fell in 1975 he defined his celebrated essay *El laberinto de la soledad (The Labyrinth of Solitude)* as moral criticism.[6]

Paz characterized these values as the clash within himself between poetry and history, often employing these terms as shorthand notions for complicated processes. For example, the nightmare of history is everything that happens that threatens individual freedom. History becomes a repressive process that dehumanizes: what has been "arrebatada / por ladrones de vida hace mil siglos" (snatched away / by thieves of life a thousand centuries ago, *P* 269). History suggests the degradation of life, the tyranny of successive time, rationality, ideologies, nationalisms, religions, science, and alienating city life. For Paz its immediate form was the period of Mexican history he grew up in. He could not avoid becoming imbued with Mexico's revitalised postrevolutionary nationalism. In his desire to become a poet in those circumstances he equated Mexican and all nationalisms as a mental disease. In the 1930s political life invaded every aspect of life. Poets were obliged to study economics, for poetry was not a useful social activity. Paz, reacting to this impinging of history on his freedom to be, became an outspoken critic of this narrow-minded authoritarian view of society (*Pe,* 66–67).

Paz came to view the revolutionary Mexican one-party system critically because he had experienced a vision of a just and free society in Spain in 1937 where the poet had a role to play and fully participated in society. Paz had witnessed the birth of the New Man there, even if briefly, before the fall of the Republic and claimed: "this memory never abandons me."[7] The ruins of this vision of the New Man haunted Paz, especially in the context of the failure of the Russian socialist revolution, the one hope of a just society for most European intellectuals in the 1920s and 1930s, but that had deeply deceived Paz, who early recoiled from Stalin's version of socialism, with its gulags and totalitarian immobility. These disappointments sharpened his moral focus about the dangers of any form of authoritarianism. In 1950 he agreed that totalitarian socialism may transform the economy of a country, but "it is doubtful if it manages to free man. And this is the only thing that interests us and that justifies a Revolution" (*L,* 152). In 1979 he confessed that much of his intellectual life had been a polemical dialogue with Marx and Marxisms, thus linking him with other dissidents (from his friendship with Victor Serge onward) who fear the way rigid ideologies control and distort history.[8]

In opposition to history the values of poetry could be synthesized to what has been called the surrealist incandescent triangle of love, liberty, and poetry.[9] In a letter in answer to an attack from a hostile

Mexican critic in 1959 Paz elaborated: "We are facing new obstacles that will not be economic but spiritual. In the industrial society such as we are beginning to glimpse all these words—art, poetry, imagination, game, love, soul, dream, analogy—shine by their absence. Man is going nowhere if it is not to find himself. The great conquest is not of outer space but of inner."[10] The values of poetry as listed by Paz become any means that can liberate man's numbed inner space.

This moral stance is not dogmatic. As a value it is determined by its plurality, its openness to life's unexpected happenings. Paz defines human nature as a personal experience manifested vividly in the here and now and irreductible to history. It is this intangible, unmeasurable, untestable extra quality that Paz explores and defends in himself. Poetry for him becomes a *saber espiritual* (spiritual knowledge), a suspicion of an alternative reality, the other shore so often evoked by Paz. Art's mission is to oppose rigid ideologies and systems, as well as the functionaries who support them, in favor of "the invincible yes of life" (*H,* 176). In this sense poetry affirms an ecstasy whose intensity of pure life abolishes history. Paz's great theme is the redemption of the divided alienated individual through love or union with the Other, a completion of the isolated individual in a passionate couple that offers hope of a collective salvation.

The active bitter conflict between poetry and history generates moments of freedom, an epiphany that Paz calls "poetic instants." Consequently, the poet's reactions to history become a test of his moral fiber. At this level Paz's desire to become a poet, to rebel against necessity and write poems without guilt, has led him to explore the functions of the poet and poem in society, both Western and Eastern, almost anthropologically. Many of his poems are explicitly about the possibility of poetry in a world that negates freedom. This desire to work out his salvation as a poet inevitably invokes the fatality of having been born a Mexican. This implies belonging to the marginalized provinces of the great empires of the twentieth century (Europe, the United States, Russia, Japan). Thus Paz's measuring himself with the world's great poets and thinkers takes on poignancy; he was not born in one of the centers of power and had to fight his way out of a limited nationalistic tradition to discover his true roots, his *mexicanidad* (Mexicannness), his contemporaneity with all who suffer history, his freedom. Paz's *vueltas* (returns) from living abroad (Spain, the United States, France, India) to Mexico have engendered his most fertile thinking about values. This moral stance, tested by the accidents of history, travel, change, love, aging, reading, and so on, supplies a remarkable coherency to the diversity of his work.

The Early Poems (1931–36) and Literary Debts

Paz published his first poem at the age of seventeen in 1931. He never collected it, but in 1982 Hugo Verani resusicated "Cabellera" (Head of hair), signed Octavio Paz Lozano, whose most revealing detail is the epigraph, in Spanish, from the French poet Saint-John Perse.[11] This epigraph suggests that French poetry sparked off Paz's career as a poet. Saint-John Perse's *Anabase* (1922) was translated by Octavio Barreda in January 1931 in the magazine *Contemporáneos* whose poets initiated Paz into modern poetry.[12]

In 1933 Paz published his first book, *Luna silvestre* (Rustic moon), in an edition of sixty-five copies, but he never reedited this slim volume. In his 1979 *Poemas (1935–75)* the initial date (1935) proclaims that his real career as a published poet began slightly later than 1933. Yet he does include dated poems written earlier: "Nocturno" (Nocturne, 1932), "Otoño" (Autumn), "Insomnio" (Insomnia, 1933), and "Espejo" (Mirror, 1934). Although Paz refused to disinter *Luna silvestre*, these earliest poems belong to the same period. Glancing through the seven poems of *Luna silvestre*, many lines and words repeat themselves as echoes from "Nocturno" *(P, 63)* from *nocturno* to *sueño* (dream), *sombra* (shadow), and *estrella* (star), as well as the use of questions "¿Cómo decir los nombres . . . ?" (How to say the names, *P, 63)* with "¿ Con qué nombre clamarte . . . ?" (With what name to call you out) in *Luna silvestre*.[13] These early poems are excessively lyrical in a Spanish purged of circumstantial details and color, of all that is nonpoetic. They are idealistic strainings to reach perfection, but they fail: "¿Cómo decir, oh Sueño, tu silencio en voces?" (How to say, O dream, your silence in voices? *P, 63)*. From this conservative Castillian language it would be hard to deduce that this is a Mexican poem. Paz was already attempting to be universal, to belong linguisticaly to a world of pure poetry without abstruse images or distorted syntax. His later poetry can be seen as a moral reaction against the false naiveties of lyrical poetry.

Paz's later poetry further reacts against excessive dependence on Rubén Darío and the Mexican poet Xavier Villaurrutia. The rhythm

and diction of lines from "Nocturno" (*P*, 63) like "Negra escala de
lirios llameantes" (Black scale of blazing irises) aptly echo Darío's
"diríase un trémulo de liras eolias" (you could say a quavering of
aeolian lyres) from "Era un aire suave" (It was a sweet tune) in *Prosas
profanas* (Profane proses, 1898).[14] There are *modernista* borrowings
in many other words ("trémula," "camelia"). The debt to Villaurrutia culminated in a book tribute by Paz called *Xavier Villaurrutia
en persona y en obra (X. V. in person and in work*, 1978). This important
Mexican debt is transparent in Paz's early poems from "Nocturno,"
whose title recalls Villaurrutia's famous "Nocturnos" published in
1928–29 in the magazine *Contemporáneos* (avidly read by Paz) and
collected in *Nostalgia de la muerte (Nostalgia for Death*, 1938). Nearly
every line from Paz's 1932 poem reveals an echo from Villaurrutia:
"sombra de las voces" (shadow of voices), "mármoles ahogados"
(drowned marble statues), "sueño" (dream), "asesinado" (assassi-
nated), and "silencio" (silence) are all associated with Villaurrutia's
magnificent "Nocturno de la estatua" (Nocturne of the statue; first
published December 1928), lucidly commented on by Paz in 1978.[15]
Just the titles of Paz's other pre-1935 poems "Espejo" and "Insomnio" evoke Villaurrutia's work. These early poems, confused with
the suppressed *Luna silvestre*, establish a position against which Paz
reacts. This position encompasses both the traditional romantic lyrical poem embodied in Darío and the poetics of the solipsistic,
isolated individual locked into his dreamscape, a metaphor of a no
place, embodied in Villaurrutia. Paz's early poetry is Mexican only
by association with Villaurrutia and his poetics of absolute interiority.

Paz's first answer to this inward, idealistic stance is political; it
comes to fruition, following his 1936 trip to Yucatán, in Spain in
1937 where he traveled with his first wife, Elena Garro, and Carlos
Pellicer. A political stance enters the once pure poems, breaking
with both the ivory-tower purity and with Villaurrutia's obsessive
self-explorations symbolized in his use of the mirror as key image.
Paz opens himself out into a dialogue with history, a feature quite
absent in Villaurrutia.

This crucial break involves Paz's debt to the generation of poets
who literary historians have grouped around *Contemporáneos*, the magazine central to Paz's education as a poet and which gave him "an
unforgetable jolt."[16] For it is Paz's differences with this group of
individuals—Villaurrutia, Gorostiza, Cuesta, Ortiz de Montellano—that allowed him to find his own voice.[17] And here a stylistic

dependence on Villaurrutia is only the surface of debts we now isolate.

(1) The *Contemporáneos* were characterized by a universalist approach to poetry and art, especially French literature: these poets disseminated, through translations and critical notes, the best world poetry of the time: Blake, Saint-John Perse, T. S. Eliot, D. H. Lawrence, Neruda, Langston Hughes, Gide, Cocteau, etc. To Julián Ríos in 1973 Paz admitted that Villaurrutia "opened the doors of modern poetry for me."[18] In 1954 Paz had thanked this generation for introducing Baudelaire, Nerval, and Blake (*Pe*, 175).

(2) Their universalist attitude implicitly denounced the cultural nationalism prevalent in Mexico during the 1920s and 1930s. Simply by affirming poetry, they went against the grain of socialist realism, the novels and memoirs of the Revolution. The same applies to their reaction against the politicized muralist painters. In Villaurrutia's case, he defended Tamayo (a defense continued polemically by Paz) and the photographer Manuel Alvárez Bravo. Villaurrutia also wrote magnificent essays on Ramón López Velarde and Sor Juana—reorientations continued and enriched by Paz who, following this lead, almost single-handedly redefined the Mexican poetic tradition, epitomized in his anthology *Poesía en movimiento* (1966).[19]

(3) Paz adopted the *Contemporáneos*'s general cultural alertness and curiosity. Exemplarily, Villaurrutia reviewed books, films, and art shows: his tastes were genuinely eclectic, spreading from Rilke (Paz wrote an uncollected piece on Rilke),[20] to Gide, Borges, Pirandello, and Valéry, even if this eclectic "intellectualism" at times annoyed Paz (*Pe*, 77).

(4) Paz differed from the *Contemporáneos* in terms of his moral intensity; he shared no wish to "escape everyday life."[21] In 1954 Paz defined this moral gap concerning the issues of the day between his generation and his predecessors as that between literary experiences (the purity of the poem) and "vital" attitudes (*Pe*, 75). Poetry had to be lived; it was a force that would transform man and destroy bourgeois society. Paz's moral imperative: "The world will be ordered according to the values of poetry—liberty and communion" (*Pe*, 78–79).

(5) This moral intensity concerning the values of poetry revealed the gap between Villaurrutia's private, anguished, oddly perverse poetic world (the bizarre images in his "Nocturno de la estatua") and Paz's own discovery of the centrality of erotic love with woman

(his other), liberty and politics. It was around politics, too prosaic
to enter a *Contemporáneos* poem, that Paz diverged. According to
Paz, Villaurrutia resented ideas, philosophy, Marxism, and current
events, while for Paz "our situation in history anguished us."[22] In
the 1930s Marxism seemed the only antidote to the catastrophic
times.

(6) Most central to Paz's debt is the way both he and Villaurrutia
before him reacted to surrealism. Both are suspicious of blind,
mindlessly automatic (mechanical) writing, yet both admitted dab-
bling with it. Both admire the claims and ideas of surrealism. Both
seek lucidity in poetry, "Keeping oneself awake," said Villaurrutia.[23] Both poets read deeply into the romantic sources of surrealism
(Blake, Nerval, Rimbaud). Paz praised Villaurrutia's "intellectual"
poems, adding: "I like the language of dreams, but mistrust dreamy
poets."[24] Paz defended this clearheadedness and in so doing confirmed his moral debt.

Paz has enumerated further debts to Villaurrutia in terms of the
craft of poetry: to curb his lyrical facility, be wary of words, and
read poetry aware of the secret nuances (*X*, 34). Paz had inherited
a wide-ranging cultural avidity from the *Contemporáneos* poets, but
found their center empty; he aspired to a more moral and political
core—interest in political events, revolution, changing man and society, Marxism, etc.

Yucatán

In 1937 Paz broke off his formal university studies—and to which
he never returned: he called himself an autodidact—in order to do
something more useful than study literature in the seclusion of a
campus. This gesture suggests a tilting of the scales in favor of
revolutionary action over reflection. Paz's dilemma centered on how
to remain a lyrical poet in such harassing times, even in revolutionary
Mexico under the most revolutionary president until then, Lázaro
Cárdenas. Going to Yucatán resolved this dilemma. Paz worked to
help implant Mexican educational policy by setting up a school in
a poor rural area near Mérida. It was social concern that led Paz
there, not a desire to study Mayan ruins. These experiences resulted
in a long poem whose final shape has dogged Paz over forty years.
Entre la piedra y la flor (Between stone and flower) was begun in
Yucatán and published in 1941. In 1976, explaining his revisions,

Paz identified his intentions as political: to show the asphixiating relationship that tied workers to the impersonal, abstract, capitalistic economy (*P, 666*).

Entre la piedra y la flor is divided into four sections. The title presupposes the peasant who lives "entre" (between) the desert— vividly evoked in images in the first section—and the flower of the sizal plant that ties him to a miserable world as exploited proletariat. The second section taps the poet's shock faced with human suffering in that stony shell of a land. The sizal's sharp-pointed leaves are opposed to this plant's sexual flower, which flowers just once in the plant's life, and compared with the flowering of human life in such harsh conditions. Section 3 centers on man immersed in this plantation land. For sizal is more than a plant: it represents a share in the stock market, man's labor, time, and sweat. The anonymous peasants wear themselves out cultivating this "abstract" plant. Paz then describes this peasant in a language reminiscent of his later *El laberinto de la soledad* (the male is polite, ceremonious, and obliging but whips his wife), and he also delves into the superstitious core of this man. Section 4 returns to money and how it controls the life-cycle. Paz develops a chain of life-denying analogies: money-wheel-number-bone-time. Certain peasant values escape the tyranny of money—the poem becomes a litany here—like their attitude to death, singing, happiness, and sorrow, their illiteracy (a wisdom ignored by money), and witchcraft. The 1976 revision conserves Paz's attack on death-giving money as the reality of those oppressed lives: an orthodox anticapitalist view (*P, 92–99*).

We will contrast the 1976 version with some of the deleted fragments, in order to catch Paz's moral/political anger of the late 1930s. The first four sections of the 1976 version are complete rewritings. In the 1941 version the peasants are addressed in the *tú* form, the comrade/brother familiarity; in the 1976 version this becomes simply man in the third person, "them" (*P, 98*). But more telling than the re-creations and new images is Paz's suppression of the fifth canto. In the original this canto leads from the poet's observations and interpretations to what action must be taken. Action, the task *(tarea)* typifies the language of those times. The poet in 1941 (1937) wanted to absorb the peasant's anger and end the capitalist world. "Para acabar con todo" (To finish everything) ends the poem; this revolutionary's *tabula rasa* is cited four times.[25] The crucial revolutionary verb *arder* (to burn) occurs ten times and points to Paz's political commitment, his "Horno invisible y puro" (Invisible and pure oven), a moral purity that later offended the poet. Paz has pruned his political revolutionary identification between the peasant's lot and the poet's task. In 1976 this conventional 1930s stance seemed ingenuous.[26]

Spain

In 1971 Paz recalled the radical Spanish poet Rafael Alberti's 1934 visit to Mexico. It was the first time that Paz heard poetry read aloud in public; he left dazzled. When Paz met Alberti in a bar he read him his own poems. Alberti commented that Paz's early poetry was not social or revolutionary, but added, "he is the only revolutionary poet among you, because he is the only one trying to transform the language."[27] That Paz still remembered Alberti's actual words is significant; it is also important that Alberti defined revolutionary poetry as seeking a revolution in language, not reflecting a revolutionary content. In 1984 Paz again returned to this 1934 encounter with the politicized Alberti. He modifies his admiration for Alberti's rather theatrical readings but again re-creates Alberti's praise for exploring his own intimacy. Paz ends: "I have never forgotten his words."[28] Alberti had guessed that Paz was not offering idealistic revolutionary rhetoric to satisfy his bad conscience.

In July 1936 Spain began her ferocious civil war. Paz, ever sensitive to current events, reacted from Mexico with a passionate poem echoing in its title the great rallying cry of the Republicans: "¡No pasarán!" (They will not pass). This circumstantial outburst has not been collected, though Paz published it in El nacional (4 October 1936) and as a pamphlet. This pamphlet has an epigraph from Elie Faure about Spain being the reality and conscience of the world. Thirty-five hundred copies were printed and all profits were ceded to the Popular Front in their "heroic" fight. The poem is an elegy that opposes human frailty and gentleness to the forces of death. Badajoz (which fell in August), Irún (fell in September), and a funerary wind are cited in a poem whose obvious protest unites it with many other poems (especially by Neruda and Vallejo) where the moral intensity and purity of the language is heightened by sharing the moral stance of the tender world of friends and comrades closing ranks against evil. The poem ends:

> Detened al terror y a las mazmorras,
> para que crezca, joven, en España,
> la vida verdadera,
> la sangre jubilosa,
> la ternura feraz del mundo libre.
> Detened a la muerte, camaradas![29]

(Stop terror and the dungeons / so that true life, / jubilant blood, / the fertile tenderness of the free world / may grow, young, in Spain. / Stop death, comrades!)

At a level of values, as a poet, Paz defended youth, the true life, love, and freedom. This poem would be hard to identify as Pazian— it appeals to a collectivity and voices a collectivity—but its moral defense of "la vida verdadera" (a phrase often used by Paz) surpasses all political creeds. If these values had socialist connotations then, Paz later shed the political husk and maintained the moral seed. The poet Efraín Huerta, reviewing this poem in 1937, thought it would "burn the reader's hands."[30]

Before finally embarking for Spain, Paz's involvement with the Spanish Republican cause and socialist politics had diverted his intimate lyric poetry into more political channels. In 1951 Paz evoked the fervor of those years: moral concepts like freedom, the people, hope, revolution shone brightly and without irony (*Pe*, 278). As if the word and the concept at last fused: the poet just had to name *pueblo* (people) and the concept became reality, the suffering Spanish people, the proletariat. As a poet, this fusion banished his alienation for the word became rooted to the thing. Simply to name was to create.

In 1937 Paz married Elena Garro and left with Carlos Pellicer for Spain, invited by Pablo Neruda to attend the second Congress of the International Association of Writers, part of the Alliance of Intellectuals in the Defence of Culture, held in Barcelona and Valencia. It was organized by Neruda from Paris (he met Paz at the station), with a secret aim (according to Hugh Thomas) to attack Gide for his critique of Russia. Some eighty writers from twenty-six countries turned up.[31]

Paz spent almost a year in Spain, but never actually fought. He said to Rita Guibert: "Spain taught me the meaning of fraternity."[32] During those hectic, thrilling, and dangerous days Paz lived out his socialist/Utopian dreams of a classless society where everybody was a poet. The intellectual poet rubbed shoulders with peasants, all equal. Paz: "Eating with those peasants during a bombardment . . . that's something I can't forget."³³ In *El laberinto de la soledad* (1950) Paz elevated this companionship (*pan*—bread: a key symbol for Paz at this experiential level) in Spain to a glimpse of full human potential realized, akin to a religious revelation. Paz: "I remember that in Spain, during the war, I had a revelation of the 'other man' and another kind of solitude . . . open to transcendence"(*L*, 23). The peasant faces Paz examined portrayed a desperate hope in a concrete and universal sense that he had *"never seen since"* (*L*, 24). Socialism shifted from a dream to a reality, the dawn of a New Man. Paz preserved this vision embodied by peasants and poets in Spain at the center of his view of the function of poetry, and he never abandoned it. This was the experiential basis to a belief that poetry restores being, awakens otherness, and transcends alienation and solitariness. Paz summarized: "In every man beats the possibility of being, or more exactly of being again, another man" (*L*, 174). In Spain he claimed (in a note on Antonio Machado whom he visited in 1938): "Liberty had become embodied" (*Pe*, 212).

That this was merely a glimpse of a potential soon crushed by Franco forms part of Paz's later rejection of a purely political revolution. He confessed to Couffon that Spain had revealed to him the impossibility of an immediate transformation of the human condition.³⁴ A sense of the ridiculousness of the intellectual's participation during those violent events emerges in Stephen Spender's memoirs *World within World* (1951). When Paz's wife suddenly burst into hysterical weeping while the children in a village danced for the poets Spender underwent "a moment of realization."³⁵ For many of the European left-wing poets the fall of Spain symbolized the end of an epoch, the collapse of all hopes about individual action against fascism exposed by Cyril Connolly: "The defeat of the Spanish Republic shattered my faith in political action."³⁶ But Paz differed; he returned to Mexico secure about possibilities for a new man, embodied in Spain in a non-Marxist revolutionary tradition.³⁷ Something had been born in Spain that would never die (*Pe*, 283).

Equally decisive for Paz in Spain was his meeting with many of his favorite poets. Not only during the Congress, but in bars, cafés, and trains he made contact with poets he had only read before: Neruda, Vallejo, Machado, Spender, Bergamín, Huidobro, Péret, Altolaguirre, and Miguel Hernández. In Spain he also first read

Luis Cernuda, a revelatory encounter. In 1942 Paz recalled his brief meetings with Miguel Hernández in Valencia, Madrid, and Paris: "days of passion and truth in which on discovering you [Hernández] and Spain, I discovered a part of myself, a rough tender root that made me greater and older" (*Pe,* 217). This revelation about his universal roots as a human being, roots older than his Mexican identity, is fundamental. He echoed this discovery in his long but severely abridged poem *Raíz del hombre* (Root of man), published in 1937. Through Hernández Paz heard (as he told Ríos) his first personal critique of Soviet Russia, for Hernández had just visited Moscow. The human aspect of his stay, the cosmopolitan congregation of writers, excited Paz. Borkenau described the babel of languages spoken, the electrical political enthusiasm, the adventure of a moral war, while Toynbee evoked a carnival atmosphere.[38] But unlike his English counterparts (Spender, Auden) Paz suffered no guilt about participating as a poet rather than as a fighter in the war.

In Spain Paz wrote and published poems. For example, his "Elegía a un joven muerto en el frente" (Elegy to a young man killed on the front), though written in Mexico in 1937, was extended in Valencia and published in *Hora de España,* a magazine "in the service of the popular cause," edited by Gil-Albert, Altolaguirre, Gaya, and Serrano Plaja who exiled themselves in Mexico and continued to collaborate with Paz. In 1979 Paz returned to the circumstances surrounding this elegy suppressed in his previous collections. He has modified aspects of the poem from its 1937 appearance. For example, the 1979 opening "Has muerto camarada / en el ardiente amanecer del mundo" (You died comrade / in the burning dawn of the world, *P,* 99) leads on to "Y brotan de tu muerte / tu mirada, tu traje azul" (And from your death / your look, your blue suit bursts out . . .); but in the 1937 we read "Y brotan de tu muerte *horrendamente vivos* / tu mirada / tu traje de *héroe*" (I have underlined the deletions: horridly alive, hero).[39] Further deletions like "crece al hombre *en puños como frutos* / puños de *combatiente y camarada*" (Grows in the man in fists like fruit / fists of a combatant and comrade) point to a toning down of the rousing political rhetoric of 1936. In a long note (1979) Paz details the ironic circumstances surrounding this elegy and names the nameless hero as José Bosch. He tells how they met, about Bosch's anarchist leanings, the two days spent in jail together, and how eventually Bosch was deported back to Spain. Then Paz read Bosch's name on a list of dead in the Civil War and thus was born his legend. Paz and his friends had a martyr (*P*, 671). In Spain in 1938, reading his poems aloud, Paz came across his old friend alive. They met and chatted before Bosch disappeared again for ever.

In Spain Paz wrote an "Oda al sueño" (Ode to dream) dated Madrid 1937, collected in 1960, then deleted;[40] an "Oda a España" (Ode to Spain) dated Madrid, Paris 1937;[41] a poem originally called "El barco" (The boat) dated Atlantic ocean 1937, presumably his boat journey to Spain which has survived as "Los viejos" (The old people) in his *Poemas*. He also edited a book *Bajo tu clara sombra y otros poemas sobre España* (Under your clear shadow and other poems about Spain) in Valencia 1937 with a note by Altolaguirre including "¡No pasarán!," his elegy and one of the odes. The title poem, dated 1935—1938 in its 1941 *Tierra nueva* edition—is a long meditative poem about words, woman, and love published during a civil war and best catches Paz's attempted fusion of an inner moral stance and change with a political one.

His "Oda al sueño" bears traces of having been written in the middle of the war in Madrid, but as a frame for a love poem, where the poet and his lover "Dormimos sobre escombros / solos entre las ruinas y los sueños" (We sleep on rubble / alone amongst the ruins and dreams)[42] of a gutted, bombed Madrid. There at night the poet discovers that the horrors of war can be redeemed by erotic love and dreaming. The poet is able to rescue his alienated, divided self: "Sueño, bajo tu manto delirante / el hombre, aniquilado, se conquista" (Dream, under your delirious cloak / man, annihilated, conquers himself).[43] The dream plunges man back into his roots, for dreams and lovers tap the "grace of eternity."[44] This experience of the redeeming dream in anguished times, of lovers re-creating a paradise in the ruins of a war "indefensos y rotos nuestros cuerpos" (our bodies defenceless and broken) exemplifies how Paz avoids any political definition of the poet's role. The poet's function is to remind his reader, his comrades, of those other inner values necessary in such vile times. Paz returned to these circumstances years later in his *Piedra de sol (Sun Stone,* 1957):

Madrid, 1937,
en la Plaza del Angel las mujeres
cosían y cantaban con sus hijos,

> después sonó la alarma y hubo gritos,
> casas arrodilladas en el polvo,
> torres hendidas, frentes escupidas
> y el huracán de los motores, fijo. . . .
>
> (*P*, 268–69)

(Madrid 1937 / in the Plaza del Angel women / were sewing and singing with their children / later when the alarm sounded there were shouts / houses kneeled in the dust / towers split, facades spat on / and the hurricane of the motors, fixed.)

During this fascist airial bombardment the lovers perform, as in his previous ode:

> los dos se desnudaron y se amaron
> por defender nuestra porción eterna,
> nuestra ración de tiempo y paraíso,
> tocar nuestra raíz y recobrarnos,
> . . . .
> porque las desnudeces enlazadas
> saltan el tiempo y son invulnerables. . . .
>
> (*P*, 269)

(the two of them stripped and made love / to defend our eternal portion / our ration of time and paradise / to touch our root and recover ourselves / because entwined nakednesses / leap over time and are invulnerable.)

Two words—*raíz* and *eterno*—link 1937 with 1957, while the values of love, defending human integrity, are made even clearer as this poem impersonalizes the lovers, interpreting erotic love as a sensation that encodes a salvation, a paradise invulnerable to history. Paz's defense against evil (the fascists who deny freedom, love, poetry) was to write a poem evoking values, not to shoot a gun. But the word "defense" links the activities at the level of social usefulness.

Paz's "El barco," later "Los viejos" (formally owing something to Pablo Neruda's "El fantasma del buque" from *Residencia en la tierra*),[45] is placed in precise circumstances, the Atlantic ocean, 1937, apparently a ship of evacuees (*P*, 102n.), fleeing fascist Spain. Or is the poem about Paz's ship *going* to Spain, with fighters going to war as a 1941 version suggests with its "van los hombres partidos por la guerra" (men set off for war)?[46] But Paz rises above his personal experience and realistic setting to invoke the moral strength of these "hombres hermosos" (fine men) who uprooted themselves to support freedom in Spain. Paz lends them natural qualities, deep voices of oranges, and cider. The 1941 poem ends: "Allí los reconozco, / allí los nombro con los ardientes nombres de mis lágrimas, / y me disuelvo en ellos y me salvo" (There I recognize them / there I name them with the burning names of my tears / and I dissolve in them and save myself). His admiration and tears of celebration for their sacrifice (a moving detail from those days) allow him to identify with them and feel saved. A reiterated notion: the fight against fascism redeemed and resolved guilt, alienation, and solitude. Paz eliminated this ending in 1979.

Paz's "Oda a España" (not collected) written in Madrid and Paris (1937) summarizes the young Paz's involvement in the Spanish Civil War. The poem explicitly deals with the "deeds of this war" and Paz's "testimonio vivo" (living testimony). All Spain speaks through him as a value embodying natural, simple, human decency. He describes his position clearly: "Sé que soy joven, . . . / pero yo quiero, amigos, camaradas, / que mis palabras, ojos, manos, lengua, . . . / hablen tan vivamente, / como esos hechos duros y gloriosos . . ." (I know I am young / but I want, friends, comrades / my words, eyes, hands, tongue / to speak as lively as those hard glorious deeds). He proclaims his awe for those young workers who sacrificed their lives and feels linked to those comrades through their spilt blood and the blood of life running through his living veins. For it is *tierra* (earth, elemental mother earth) that speaks through all of the participants the values of peace and love. Paz's insight is that Adam, the New Man, was being reborn in Spain (see note 41).

It is at this level of love (blood, earth, human voice: the analogies are deliberately archetypal and obvious) that we can read *Bajo tu clara sombra,* written in Mexico in 1935 but published in Spain during the war. In its original version it is a long elegy in ten cantos celebrating words, love, prehistory, woman, man, and the natural world. Paz felt these values needed affirming during the Civil War, experienced as a moral crusade against the forces of evil. The poem justifies the necessity of poetry, man's inner purity, love, and all that unites man and woman with life: "la palabra del goce de la tierra" (the word of pleasure of the earth).[47] Pax celebrates man's innocence: "y tornamos a ser tierra inocente, / y el aire, en los

espacios, / madura desnudez y libertad" (and we become innocent
earth again, / and air, in the spaces, / matures nakedness and liberty). The function of poetry is to recall man's real nature: "me
desnudan de mí" (they strip me of myself), a nature deeper than
ego, personality, and history. This experience occurs in the present
tense of the act of love:

> donde vibra el instante,
> la frenética música:
> la cima de los besos,
> la plenitud del mundo y de sus formas.

(Where the instant vibrates / the frantic music: / the peak of kisses, /
plenitude of the world and its forms.)

The poet allows himself to be the channel of this natural upsurge
where words are compared to sap rising up the stalk/throat (Paz
returns to this image in *Blanco, White/target*, 1966) for the poet is
spellbound by life (Paz had been reading Nietzsche at the time).
Paz defended this version of harmony and integrity in a war. This
is the poem's real context.[48]

Paz's scant poems dealing with this formative period in his life
do not seem overtly political, but in this specific historical context
and dilemma, they do defend values. And they concern "man," not
Mexican man. Paz said to Couffon that during the Civil War he
explored the problem of contemporary man.[49] It was a crisis period
in Western history. Juan Gil-Albert reviewed *Bajo to clara sombra*
in *Hora de España* in 1937 stressing the difference in Paz between
the real poet and propaganda. Paz has not confused passion for a
cause with poetry; he concludes: "when a young man writes these
poems in which life shines out, he is, for the mere fact of having
written them, on the side of the revolution that men desire."[50]

Return to Mexico

Paz returned to Mexico via Paris in 1938, determined to continue
the fight against fascism and not too disillusioned over the collapse
of the Popular Front. Paz supported Lázaro Cárdenas's official policy
of welcoming all Republicans to Mexico and refusing recognition
of Franco's dictatorship. From 1938 Paz wrote a daily article on

political events for the left-wing newspaper *El popular*, gave speeches in favor of the cause, and founded a literary magazine *Taller* (Workshop,)1938–41 with militant overtones that had an open-doors policy for the Spanish exiles, to such an extent that Rafael Solanas called it a Spanish magazine edited in Mexico, displacing Mexicans, while Abreu Gómez chided that it should concern itself with the Mexican Revolution: *"Taller* must finish the ideological work of the Revolution."[51] The magazine ran to twelve numbers with Paz editing numbers 5 to 12. It was essentially a literary review.

In his own review Paz published the poems "Noche de resurrecciones" and the "Oda al sueño," and over the period 1938–42 he increased his critical output in prose as a complementary side to being a poet, as if he needed prose to sort out and define his position. A crucial encounter for Paz was with the exiled Spanish poet León Felipe. In 1938 he wrote a "Saludo a León Felipe" (A greeting to L. F.) in which he insisted that Mexicans recognize their links with the Spaniards and discover their full humanity (*Pe*, 194). In 1939, in *Taller*, Paz wrote "El mar" (The sea), an eulogistic review of Felipe's *El hacha* (The axe), a book Paz called "the spiritual history of Spanish man."[52] Paz explains what a poet makes of the accidents of politics (the Spanish Civil War): "a poet gathers the historical experience and converts it via poetry into a metaphysical experience," what Paz himself did and a socially justifiable and important activity.[53] Felipe's "blasphemy" prolonged the view current then that Spain was the world's bad conscience, the loss of its pure voice a crime shared by all. Paz as a Mexican whose government actively helped particularly blamed the Western democracies. In 1971 Paz told Julián Ríos that it was Felipe's moral attitude to the world rather than his actual poems that so moved him. León Felipe embodied the Spanish cause.

Already in his *Taller* poem "Noche de resurrecciones," with its romantic hint of rebirth through night, Paz had begun his separation from explicit political circumstances in a poem whose value lay in its insistence on origins, dream, and the night, a world of "hacia dentro" (toward the inside) seeking the sources of love. It continues the themes and treatment of *Bajo tu clara sombra* and meditates on what is universal and eternal in all men. In an age of feuds, cataclysms, and world wars a search for some transcendent refuge, a "solitaria llama" (solitary flame) makes sense.[54] The poem is collected and abbreviated in *Poemas* (1979).

Paz himself has made much of what he called the *Taller* generation. He became their spokesman, but without Paz, this generation is not as varied or rich as the *Contemporáneos* grouping of poets. We see the *Taller* group as a modification and underscoring of what the *Contemporáneos* stood for embodied in one person, Octavio Paz. In a 1963 interview Paz confirmed this view by stressing the *Contemporáneos* poets as "exemplary masters of rebellion" opening Mexican letters to the new poetry and beginning a tradition of criticism that culminates in Paz.[55] In 1982 a facsimile edition of *Taller* appeared, and in 1983 Paz published a memoir about his participation in the magazine (*S*, 94–113). The main difference between the generations centered on left-wing politics; the name *Taller*, workshop, craft, community, explains the intentions best. By 1983 Paz regards this political tendency with shame, and his memoir is a *mea culpa* confessing his blindness to Stalin and Russia. It is ironic that Paz also admits his antipathy to André Breton's clear-sighted break with the Stalinists in 1930 when by 1947 he had befriended Breton and shared his "moral indignation" with left-wing totalitarianism.

As well as collaborating with Spanish exiles in *Taller*, Paz also edited a small anthology of contemporary Spanish verse called *Voces de España* (1938), that commemorates the second anniversary of their "heroic fight." In a letter published in *Letras de México* (1938) Paz explained that he wished to keep alive the spirit that sacrificed itself for "human freedoms" in those poets who actually fought for Spain (and thus excluding Salinas and Aleixandre).[56]

In 1941 Paz coedited with Xavier Villaurrutia, Emilio Prados, and Juan Gil-Albert an anthology of modern poetry in Spanish entitled *Laurel*. This anthology reflected Paz's and that period's perception that the Spanish language and tradition was one, a fraternity of poets whose true nationality was a common language. Paz recently returned to the editing of this anthology in a long essay entitled "Poesía e historia" (Poetry and history). This intellectual autobiography describes some of the minor scandals of that time, especially Pablo Neruda's refusal to allow his poems to appear. But *Laurel*'s purpose was still political: solidarity with the fallen Republic (*S*, 47–93).

Over those years following his return from Spain Paz published essays on Rilke, poetry and mythology, history and philosophy, and a series of semidiary but impersonal jottings on art, metaphysics, myth, desire, religion in a Nietzschean, and aphoristic form that

owes something also to the apocryphal philosophers / teachers
Abel Martín and Juan de Mairena invented by Antonio Machado.
These began in *Taller* (1938) as "Vigilias" (Night work), subtitled
"Diary of a dreamer" and continued in other magazines—*Tierra nueva,
El hijo pródigo*—up to 1945. Here Paz meditated in prose what he
worked on in verse, an overlapping that has continued throughout
his life. For example, on the pressing question What is poetry in
the context of a world war?, Paz wrote in prose: "Poetry is innocence,
but the poet is not innocent. Thus his anguish; poetry is a grace,
a gift but also a thirst and a suffering. Poetry springs from pain
like water from earth. With poetry the poet recovers his innocence,
remembers a Lost Paradise and bites into the old apple. But what
tough waste-lands, what deserts he must cross to get to the front!"[57]
In Mexico in 1940 Paz wrote a poem "La poesía" dedicated to Luis
Cernuda (this dedication was removed in 1979) where "Poetry" is
a purifying force that invades the poet, makes him "naked, stripped"
(that is, innocent). Poetry is a burning truth, an "avidity" (a thirst)
and is indestructible. It arises from his depths, his being, and makes
the poet prophetic. Poetry is the "unity of his soul and body" (a
Lost Paradise). This poem harks back to Paz's "Oda al sueño." When
poetry, the muse, touches the poet he recognizes his true nature,
his identity, his link with nature, mother, reality: "unta mis ojos
con aceite, / para que al conocerte me conozca" (anoint my eyes
with oil, / so that on recognizing you I recognize myself, *P,* 106).
Paz's stress on innocence during a foul world war becomes his metaphor for a state outside history, ideology, and language that resolves
guilt and alienation yet affirms a belief in human potential and the
poet's role. This innocence has a Nietzschean ring.[58]

In *Taller* Paz had affirmed that the poet "is the conscience of
existence."[59] This phrase underscores the notion that Paz's ques-
tionings go beyond the forms of poetry or prose to find their origins
in an ethical stance. Paz's first article was tellingly titled "Ética del
artista" (Artist's ethics, 1931). His dialogue with the history of
those days lies inside his poems, invisibly, in his desperate insistence
on innocence.[60]

Paz's meditational fragments "Vigilias" continued in 1941 with
further thoughts on man's double or triple nature, a self-dialogue
between history and poetry within the poet. Here Paz began his
exploration of *soledad* (solitude) that culminated in his appendix to
El laberinto de la soledad (1959). This exploration of *soledad* became

the driving force of Paz's thinking over the next eighteen years. Paz: "I want to find the deepest voice inside me . . . the insoluble solitude of a creature, evidence of man's eternal solitude."[61] This concept and experience of *soledad,* fruitfully studied by one of Paz's earliest and best critics, Ramón Xirau,[62] obsessed the *Contemporáneos* poets, but derives from Paz's thorough reading of Nietzsche— Paz: "Only Nietzsche is capable of comfort"[63]—also indicates the beginning of the poet's isolation from a political collaborative role fighting the nightmare of history. During this period following the Civil War (1941 on) Paz became marginalized and disillusioned with his earlier political enthusiasm about changing man and society.

This burgeoning crisis concerns what Paz calls the "moral sense," man's sixth sense, equated with guilt. Paz explored this sense in relation to freedom, nature, integrity, and sexuality. He defined this sense in D. H. Lawrence terms as a religion. Much of his later thinking develops from these crucial years. He saw left-wing politics as a disguised religious longing but as yet was not critical of this: "Its end is communion: thus it does not aim to create a morality but a religion (this is nothing other than the deep aim of communism, which seeks fraternity, the active communion of desperate people, as well as of the disinherited)."[64] Still, in 1941 left-wing fraternity held a positive connotation in Paz's personal quest for communion, resolving his own guilt and emptiness as a poet. Paz identified with the "desesperados" of those war years.

In these 1941 fragments Paz included a lyrical paragraph about his muse's or lover's eyes. During those same years he also wrote a poem "Tus ojos" (Your eyes) published in *Libertad bajo palabra* (Liberty under parole, 1949), undated, in the section "El girasol" (Sunflower, 1943–48). The poem is one long conceit. It opens with "Tus ojos son" (Your eyes are) and continues with sixteen lyrical analogies for "her" eyes, as if poetry can only approximate the reality of her eyes. There are crucial overlaps with the prose piece that help date the poem.

In the prose "her" eyes open and devour the poet. He plunges into these eyes and sinks into a magical world, like a sea, where he experiences such intensity that life and death, solitude and company fuse. He loses his name, his illusory individuality, and becomes naked but full of life. He has experienced "our deepest, most ungraspable condition."[65] The poem also has her eyes drawing the poet into a marvelous inscape with a sea (watery eyes). Here eyes are "puertas del más allá" (doors to the beyond, *P*, 125), an absolute. The difference between the pieces is that the prose explains while the poem enthuses through images. For abstract "plenitude" in the prose, we read in the poem "pájaros presos, doradas fieras adormecidas, / topacios impíos como la verdad" (trapped birds, golden sleeping beasts, / topazes pitiless as the truth, *P*, 125). In the prose the revelation is awkwardly "unsayable,' in the poem it is sayable: "pulsación tranquila del mar a mediodía" (the sea's midday tranquil pulsation, *P*, 125). Both prose and poem create a passionate edifice of words around an erotic experience, both affirm love as the only alternative to politics, history, and the corrupt world. Both are secret tributes to Paul Eluard (cf. "L'Amoureuse," 1924; "Avec tes yeux").[66]

Historical events began to sour Paz's belief in the efficacy of political idealism. The 1940 Hitler-Stalin pact, the totalitarian nature of the Soviet regime (but not its gulags, nor its persecutions of dissidents) and the 1940 assassination of Trotsky (Paz: "it horrified me,"*S*, 110) increased Paz's despair about the world situation. The squabbles between rival splinter groups about socialist realism or the duties of the writer and friendship with dissidents like Victor Serge (who put Paz on to the revelatory work of Henri Michaux; Paz to Ríos: "a discovery of capital importance for me") forced Paz to retreat from active politics and "history" as the stage for social change. Paz: "I could break the spell" (that Marxist revolutions held over him, *S*, 108). He began a period of intense isolation. He told Scherer about this break: "I was left very alone" (*O*, 328). Paz turned inward and from late 1943 left Mexico for over eleven years. Over these years of self-imposed exile and search for new horizons poetry came more and more to represent the only moral value in a world in ruins.

One incident summarized Paz's break with party politics and concerned Pablo Neruda. Similar to many of his generation, Paz's discovery of Neruda was a revelation. Whether Paz obtained the books (he still owns a first edition of *Residencia en la tierra* [Residence on earth], 1933) or read individual poems in *Contemporáneos* in 1931, does not alter his shocked thrill of reading a poet from his own culture and continent. Paz to Ríos: "For me Neruda was the great destructer-creator of Hispanic poetry."

We suggested that Paz's 1937 "El barco" ("Los viejos") owes its topic— a boat—and its buildup of sensual, approximate images to Neruda. But Neruda's stylistic influence is not visible until some of Paz's 1940s poems. Paz met Neruda in Paris in 1937. Neruda had invited him over to the Congress on the strength of Paz's first book of 1933.[67] As well as his poems Paz had also avidly read Neruda's literary magazine *Caballo verde para la poesía* (Green horse for poetry), sharing his attack on Juan Ramón Jiménez's pure poetry. On his return from Spain in 1938, in an uncollected piece "Pablo Neruda en el corazón" (P. N. in the heart) Paz confessed that Neruda had excitingly reintroduced *lo real* (reality) into a poetry that had become overpurified.[68] Paz identified with this attack on a poetry that expressed "horror for all nonessential reality."[69] Paz labeled these idealistic poems "beautiful refrigerators" while Neruda's poetry was a "living conquering flow," that is, life, a plunging into the depths of sonorous matter itself. Neruda had created not a mimetic poetry, but a poetry whose images and metaphors had become as solid as reality. Paz praises Neruda's Civil War poems (*España en el corazón* [Spain in the heart]; cf. the title of Paz's piece) because it tapped the same sources as Marx, but poetically: "the purest spring of human work."[70] This "purest," a moral concept, shows that Paz and Neruda shared values (in 1938), and these values coalesced in Spain, not only a political/historical issue but the "decisive fact of our moral history" where man touched his roots, his essence, the great metaphysical drama of time and nothingness.[71] Neruda's poetry incited to continued action in order to defend this value from the subhuman *cloaca* (sewer) of fascism. It is evident why Paz refused to collect this "document" of his political ambitions of then.

But in 1941 Paz feuded with Neruda who was consul general for Chile in Mexico. The feud began with Neruda's refusal to let his poems be published in Paz's coedited anthology *Laurel*. It involved Neruda's antipathy to José Bergamín, a meal in honor of Neruda's departure, and how Neruda and Paz nearly came to blows and did not speak to each other until they met in London in 1967 (*S*, 54–56). In many ways, Neruda's person and poetry came to embody all the dogmatic partisanship that began to embitter Paz. Paz's response to Neruda was virulent. And Neruda blamed this vitriolic quality as endemic to Mexican literary life. In his memoirs Neruda wrote: "Woe to anybody who from the outside takes side in favor of or against one or other group."[72] It is true that Paz (like Neruda) has been involved in other public feuds, due perhaps to his moral stance but never as intransigently as André Breton.

Paz's "Respuesta a un cónsul" (Answer to a consul), which appeared in *Letras de México* in 1943, accused Neruda's friends in Mexico of being "lackeys" and Neruda's poetry of being "contaminated" by politics, of being confused and possessing a "titanic" vanity. Paz lists three points of attack on Neruda. The first concerns the ineptitude of political poetry: poetry cannot cause a political change, better a text by Lenin than bad poems by Mayakovsky or Neruda. Paz repeated his attack on Neruda's vanity, bitterness, and access to "money" that allowed him to give dinners to the *jauría* (pack of hounds) of Mexican intellectuals that adulated him. All this because Neruda had dared accuse Mexican poets of a lamentable "lack of civil morality."[73] By 1943 Paz had clearly separated the poet from the political activists, resisting the attempt to unite both under the banner of revolution. His attack on Neruda was equally directed against Mexicans. In 1959 Paz told Couffon: "From the moral point of view [Neruda] seems to me to be the living example of the poet degraded by a party."[74]

Paz published "La poesía" (Poetry, 1940), dedicated to Luis Cernuda, in *A la orilla del mundo* (On the world's shore, 1942), which collected most of his poems up to that date. As stated, the 1979 *Poemas* deleted both date and dedication. Paz's first reading of Cernuda's poetry in Civil War Spain hinted at his later development away from politics but remaining firmly faithful to an ethic (like Cernuda). What most impressed Paz about Cernuda (as he said to Ríos) was that Cernuda's "moral subversion was united with a poetic subversion and that it was impossible to identify a social revolution with a poetic subversion." Paz has always acknowledged his debt to Cernuda, especially in his magnificent essay "La palabra edificante" (The edifying word) written in 1964 and published in *Cuadrivio* (Quadrivium, 1965), exploring this moral, dissident dimension. Cernuda settled later in Mexico and befriended Paz. In 1958 Paz highlighted Cernuda's consciouness of his position in the world as a poet. Cernuda's work challenged orthodox values, and Paz had discovered in Cernuda something absent in all the other poets of that generation (i.e., Neruda): "The consciousness of the poet's destiny as being a person apart and who only affirms his self by negating the abject world that surrounds him."[75] In 1962 Paz commemorated his friend in a poem "Luis Cernuda 1902–1963" (the dates added in 1979) where Cernuda becomes prototypic, "el poeta" (the poet, *P*, 323–25).

The 1940 dedicated poem describes poetry as an inner value, activity, and experience that gives the poet his identity: "Entre mis ruinas me levanto, / solo, desnudo, despojado" (Among my ruins I raise myself, / alone, naked, stripped, *P*, 104). This purifying experience from the ruins and collapse of Paz's political faith in change is linked to Cernuda's *deseo* (desire), the title of his collected poetry *La realidad y el deseo* (Reality and desire); the poet's inner avidity or thirst that is never quenched. Only through this burning integrating experience can Paz open his eyes on to the world and reality. Man without "poetry" (desire) would become a puppet of history, a hollow man. Poetry had become a faith (a fate), an "ardiente balbuceo" (burning stuttering, *P*, 105), his "madre mía" (my mother, *P*, 106), a muse that obliges the poet to remain faithful to her vision. This was Cernuda's exemplary quality, just the direction that Paz sought in his confusions of the 1940s. In war ravaged Europe there can be no political revolution. The poet is a loner.

In the poem "Delicia" (Delight), dedicated to José Luis Martínez, a critic who supported Paz's attack on Neruda with a note, published in *A la orilla del mundo* (1942), Paz inserted poetry into a bureaucratic, party political context:

> Entre conversaciones y silencios,
> lenguas de trapo y de ceniza,
> entre las reverencias, dilaciones,
> las infinitas jerarquías,
> los escaños del tedio,
> los bancos del tormento,
> naces, delicia, alta quietud.
> (*P*, 40)

(Between conversations and silences, / tongues of rag or ash, / between reverences, delays, / the benches of torment, / you are born, delight, high stillness.)

In earlier editions Paz explicitly wrote "naces, poesía" ("you are born, poetry," not "delicia"). He also deleted the last lines of the stanza, which read: "y danzas, invisible, frente al hombre. / El presidio del tiempo se deshace" (and you dance, invisible, before

man / The prison of time is undone, *Li,* 33). The poem has shed
an explicitness (1979) necessary in 1942. It articulates an alternative
"lost paradise" that redeems the poet from fawning party politics
and its corrupt dead language, the nontranscendental banalities of
such meetings. Poetry had become the only experience able to liberate man from the tyranny of history (time).

During the 1940s, as Paz moved away from the spell of left-wing
politics, a critical myth about Paz emerged. It stated that Paz had
betrayed his lucidly clear lyrics. The more he became involved with
surrealism as the only viable moral stance to take in the middle of
the twentieth century, the more critics vociferated against the rising
obscurity in his poetry. Paz knew that moral idealism need not of
necessity flow into party politics, but his poetry is only political if
we separate the poetry from the lucid self-conscious moral contexts
that he has elaborated in his dialogue with his age.

From being the darling of the left-wing poets (cf. Alberti's and
Neruda's early admiration), Paz had drifed into obscurity. In 1941
Abreu Gómez had praised Paz's *Entre la piedra y la flor* as one of
the most deeply felt, human, responsible poems ever written in
Mexico.[76] In 1958 Salazar Mallén wrote of Paz's early promise claim-
ing that Paz became exhausted by 1940, a poet of works of inferior
quality.[77] In 1965 Raúl Leiva contrasted the early clear, naked,
distant poems with the illogicality and hermeticism of Paz's 1950s
work.[78] Finally, E. Carballo (with whom Paz feuded in 1959) wrote
in 1967 that Paz who knew how to separate poetry from propaganda
had silenced himself and become deaf and blind to what happens
socially and politically in the world.[79] But all these Mexican critics
confused party politics with an ethical stance.

Chapter Two

The Surrealist Years: 1943–53

The United States

Paz abandoned the political rivalries of Mexico with a Guggenheim scholarship for a two-year stay in the Mexican enemy of the north, the United States. He traveled around the continent (San Francisco, Los Angeles, New York), slowly working out his identity as a Mexican poet in the shadow of the European war, dissatisfied with a political revolution as a means of changing man and society. Living through this distant terrible war and its effect on questions of purpose, identity, and value was inevitably confusing. We could phrase the dilemma thus: could Paz find a substitute to his political activity that had tried to fuse the individual into a collectivity, without falling back into the romantic error of the marginalized solitary lyric poet? Over these years Paz insisted on a communal solution to individual alienation. It is at this level of quest that the brotherhood of surrealists, governed by André Breton's intransigent ethical stance, became a viable alternative that bound the poet to social change. But in the 1940s it was still Luis Cernuda's brand of surrealism concerning the poet's destiny as a "profoundly individual" subversion that helped Paz grow. During those years Paz turned more and more toward poetry, meeting poets like E. E. Cummings, Robert Frost, Jorge Guillén, and William Carlos Williams, and reading or translating Pound, Wallace Stevens, T. S. Eliot, and José Juan Tablada.

When Paz first read T. S. Eliot's "The Hollow Men" and *The Waste Land*, translated by León Felipe and Enrique Mungía respectively, in *Contemporáneos* in 1930 and 1931,[1] he suffered an unforgettable jolt. As the editor of *Taller* Paz followed up this discovery with a supplement *Poemas de T. S. Eliot* (1940) with translations by Angel Flores, Rodolfo Usigli, and Ortiz de Montellano, among others.[2] In 1984 Paz explained why his reading of Eliot in translation

27

in Mexico so affected him: Eliot represented "modernity," his pur-
gatory (*The Waste Land*) grappled with the modern world not as a
metaphysical nor psychological poem but as a historical reality itself
(*S*, 101–2). Paz admired Eliot's example of transmuting bitter historical experience into a liberating poem. Eliot voiced the spiritual
aridity of the twentieth century: "Modern man is a character from
Eliot. Everything is alien for him and he recognizes himself in
nothing. It's an expiation. Man is not a tree, nor a plant nor a bird.
He is alone in the middle of creation" (*A*, 79). Paz later called this
Eliot's religious vision of modern Western history. If we read that
quotation into Paz: in the 1940s he embodied this expiation of
guilt, sterility, and alienation, consciously, in a hostile world. The
waste land voiced his experiences of history. And to be conscious
of this was the beginning of exorcizing it.

That Paz inherited this vision from a poet strengthened his belief
in the efficacy and importance of poetry in a world set on eradicating
it as a value. And what distinguishes the poet from the crowd centers
on his consciousness of this dilemma. A crucial text coloring those
years and preparing Paz for his realization that poetry can lead to
a community, through the surrealists, is his much-commented-on
1942 essay "Poesía de soledad y poesía de comunión" (Poetry of
solitude and poetry of communion). The historical context of this
lecture is his disenchantment with the magic word "revolution" and
his seeking salvation from being a hollow man through poetry.

The essay opens with the notion that reality is far richer, more
variable and alive than any system that tries to explain it; Paz
probably has in mind Marxism and all forms of scientific interpretations. He then outlines an alternative approach to knowing reality:
love, a dissolution of the self in the other, a nostalgia for roots, the
psychic place of rebirth. In Spain Paz had located his ancient bitter
roots. But lovers descend more vertiginously to this ancient pure
animal energy. And poetry is like love, a dialogue with the world,
oscillating between solitude and communion, a *salto mortal* (mortal
leap) back to man's paradisaical nature. Paz differentiates poetry
from conservative religion as being a dissident marginalized indi-
vidualistic knowledge (cf. Cernuda). Paz's answer in 1942 to left-
wing politics is an anarchistic heterodoxy where poetry reveals man's
innocence, consecrating in language man's relations with the world,
woman, his consciousness. Poetry: "testimonio del éxtasis" (witness
of ecstasy, *Pe*, 125). Consequently, most societies, especially capi-

talism, condemn this knowledge called poetry. Paz ends by inserting this dissident poetics into a social context: "Poetry, expressing these dreams, invites us to rebel, to live our dreams awake, to be not the dreamers but the dream itself" (*Pe,* 132). These notions end his later *El laberinto de la soledad.* Central here is Paz's need to enact his poetics and remain conscious of this drive. In the 1940s the poet becomes the real hero and outbids the revolutionary by changing himself before changing society and enlarging that inner life denied by Marxism. The poet's heroic act is lucidity in a dark age.

Pondering these ambitious notions, steeping himself in Anglo-Saxon poetry, Heidegger, and the surrealist tradition, Paz also gained an insight into American capitalism and his own identity as a poet and Mexican. Being abroad invisibly clarified his Mexican roots in ways that would have been impossible had he stayed on in Mexico. Paz's identification with the *Pachucos* (chicanos) of Los Angeles initiated his inquiry into what it meant to be a Mexican after the Revolution, within the broader context of an alienated twentieth century. Sympathizing with the stateless *Pachuco* and fusing his feelings of being marginalized by history with these outcasts generated the fine opening chapter of his later *El laberinto de la soledad.*

Paz collected the poems corresponding to these errant years in *Libertad bajo palabra* (1949). "Niña" (Girl), first published in 1943 but extensively rewritten in 1979 and dedicated to his daughter from his first marriage, blends the girl with his muse and her capacity to infuse reality with revelation. She names. She embodies a poetry that "nos alza a plenitudes / nos vuelve a ser nosotros, extraviados" (raises us to plenitudes / returns us to being ourselves, lost, *Li,* 37) in a direct language, without recourse to images, close to his 1942 prose.

The section "Puerta condenada" (Blocked door) in *Libertad bajo palabra* that contains most of the *soledad* or frustration poems exploring Paz's dilemmas of the 1940s also includes his North American ones. "El muro" (The Wall; cf. Cernuda's "un muro, ¿no comprendes? / un muro frente al cual estoy solo"—a wall, don't you understand / a wall in front of which I am alone—from "Telarañas cuelgan de la razón"),[3] first published in 1943, testifies to Paz's assumption of Eliot's waste land within himself, adrift in a hostile world without room for a poet. The poem glosses Cernuda's poem from 1931: love is a lie; revelation and ecstasy an empty promise. The wall blocking reality out locks the poet within himself.

A rich inscape does not suffice: "Cierro los ojos: nacen dichas, goces, / bahías de hermosura, eternidades" (I close my eyes: happiness, pleasures / bays of beauty, eternities are born, *Li*, 6). The poem ends with a plea for release from the desert of the alienated self:

> Mas cierra el paso un muro y todo cesa.
> Mi corazón a oscuras late y llama.
> Con puño ciego y árido golpea
> la sorda piedra y suena su latido
> a lluvia de ceniza en un desierto.
>
> (*Li*, 67)

(But a wall closes the passage and all ceases. / My heart in darkness beats and calls. / With blind, arid fist it beats / the deaf stone and its heartbeat sounds / like a rain of ash in the desert.)

The last derivative line combines both Eliot and Cernuda in "ash" and "desert." But Paz's poem documents a lament for the absence of the liberating other. It is more literary than Cernuda's "Telarañas . . ." but also more desperate for a lover, a muse. The poem epitomizes Paz's break in the 1940s with politics. It was not collected in the 1979 *Poemas*.

In the 1940s there are few poems about liberation, living one's dream awake and transfusing inert matter through the powers of the mind. An exception is the last section of "Conscriptos U.S.A." where stones become bread, paper sea gulls, fingers birds thanks to poetry "todo vuela" (all flies). But this poem follows the 1942 prose essay by describing how poetry should work; like a manifesto it promises but does not really convey or convince (*P*, 80).

The experiential truth of that period was alienation, as in "Seven P.M." (first published 1945) where the poet mocks rush-hour mentality in an artificial city (New York), ruled by clock time, not desires (Cernuda again). The city dwellers, denizens of Eliot's waste land, "condenados solitarios" (solitary condemned people), smile, read newspapers, unaware. The muse interrupts the poem with her song of a better, richer, more natural life. The poem ends on a note of black humor, the poet reacting to the time-is-money syndrome: "doblan la esquina, puntuales, Dios y el tranvía" (punctually turning the corner, God and a tram, *P*, 84).

Another city poem about urban anguish is "La calle" (The street), published in 1945, where the poet trips along with blind feet over dumb stones, followed by his divided self who evaporates when confronted. A neat poem about the persecution mania of the isolated poet, excluded from a meaningful community during the horror of the war. The city becomes a metaphor as it did for Eliot of a labyrinth of solitude with nobody recognizing anybody: the seed for Paz's later theory of the *ninguneo* (nobodying) prevalent in urban societies:

> donde nadie me espera ni me sigue,
> donde yo sigo a un hombre que tropieza
> y se levanta y dice al verme: nadie.
>
> (*P*, 85)

(where nobody waits for me or follows me, / where I follow a man who stumbles / lifts himself up and says on seeing me: nobody.)

"Cuarto de hotel" (Hotel room) further evokes Eliot's restless, mindless, transient man and continues this 1940s vein of despair: a world of hollows, shadows, nothingnesses (*P*, 85–87). But it is the ending of "Elegía interrumpida" (Interrupted elegy) that summarizes Paz's mood: "Es un desierto circular el mundo, / el cielo está cerrado y el infierno vacío" (the world is a circular desert / heaven is closed and hell empty, *P*, 89).

The best poem that articulates Paz's despair in the United States during the war is "Soliloquio de medianoche" (Midnight soliloquy), with long, flowing lines, an anecdote, and conversations where the freer form contrasts with the mood of anger and despair, except that the poem deals with the consciousness of this state, and that in itself is liberating. It is dated Berkeley 1944 and is much altered in its 1979 version. The title catches the isolation of a poet talking to himself alone in the middle of the night where night becomes a metaphor of the times. Paz, the romantic idealist who had touched his ancient roots and primal innocence in Spain, has become trapped in his little room, a "roedor civilizado" (civilized rodent, *P*, 112). The poet overhears the taunts about others fighting and kissing in the world (political involvement, the war). Insomniac, defeated, he despairs of all values (though his anger is an energy):

> creí que al fin la tierra me daba su secreto,
> pechos de viento para los desesperados,

elocuentes vejigas ya sin nada:
Dios, Cielo, Amistad, Revolución o Patria.
                                                        (*P, * 113)

(I thought that at last the earth gave me its secret, / breasts of wind for desperate men, / eloquent bladders now empty: / God, Heaven, Friendship, Revolution or Mother Country.)

These idealist hopes for change or security now empty bladders, a *mea culpa* for having believed (in God, then Revolution). This poem's tone suggest the surrealist influence of Cernuda's poems like "¿Son todos felices?" or "Diré como nacisteis": "Adonde no llegan realidades vacías / leyes hediondas, códigos, ratas de paisajes derruidos" (where empty realities do not reach / stinking laws, codes, rats of demolished landscapes).[4]

Even the poet's magical infancy ("savage innocence"), where once the natural poet's magic words could open the doors of heaven, is over, meaningless in 1944. The exiled, lost poet recalls a childhood tree thick with birds, a bougainvillea, a fountain, flowers, a fig tree (later to become Paz's emblem for the grace of childhood). All this magical world sold "por unas baratijas de prudencia" (for the baubles of prudence, *P,* 114), *prudencia,* another Cernudian pet hate word. All the poet's dreams of a recuperative love and political glory crashed, a desert. The archetypal dream expounded in 1942 where "la palabra engendraría / y el mismo sueño habría sido abolido" (the word would engender / and the very dream would have been abolished, *P,* 114) has lead to the dead end of the poet "a solas" (alone, *P,* 114). As we would expect, he is particularly guilty about those fighting (the Allies in Europe) and dying "por defender una palabra, / llave de sangre para cerrar o abrir las puertas del Mañana" (to defend a word / key of blood to close or open the doors of Tomorrow, *P,* 115). The defended word is, of course, freedom. But to Paz in 1944 this was pointlessly spilt blood, for nothing had changed:

Sangre para bautizar la nueva era que el engreído profeta vaticina,
sangre para el lavamanos del negociante,
sangre para el vaso de los oradores y los caudillos. . . .
                                                        (*P,* 115)

(Blood to baptize the new era predicted by the vain prophet, / blood for the businessman's washbasin, / blood for the orators and leaders's glasses.)

All this blood spilt (capitalist crimes, Stalin's dreams, the Mexican revolution) culminated in "yermos" (waste lands, *P,* 115). Paz's nausea with political action has reached pit bottom. The empty politicians of both sides, socialist and capitalist, have cast the poet aside. In 1944 the poet saw no alternative hope, no substitute mode of action. An eternal night, with a dead sun in an empty dream: all that remained of his potent 1930s dreams.

Paris

Libertad bajo palabra (1949), as its title implies, ends with several exciting poems written once Paz was installed in Paris as cultural attaché for Mexico. This official position did not prevent Paz from befriending André Breton and the postwar surrealist group, probably the most absorbing and influential friendship in Paz's life as a poet. To assess the relief of this debt we need only invoke the two years in the United States deflected from left-wing politics, dedicated to poetry and Paz's resent with the lone voice, the lyrical poet's isolation in the war years. This surrealist group, dominated by Breton, and its moral activities based on erotic love and poetry, appealed to Paz's need to belong to a group and seek communal solutions to his age's dilemmas. Albert Camus summarized Breton's role in the 1940s: "In the foul times of his age, and this cannot be forgotten, he is the only one to have spoken deeply about love."[5] Breton's example: how to remain a poet in such an awful historical moment, illuminated and confirmed Paz's own mission as a poet. From 1945 to 1951 (and more briefly during 1959–62) Paz lived in Breton's Paris, one of his select group.

Before evaluating Paz's debts to Breton within his works, one crucial context favored Paz, reversing a cultural trend of Paris worship embodied in Paz's Latin American poet predecessors (especially Rubén Darío). Although Paris and the French poetic tradition (Rimbaud, Lautréamont, Apollinaire) had always been the poetic tradition to emulate and compete with, Paz had arrived in 1945 in a Paris recently occupied, in the grim poverty of the early postwar years, with rationing, recriminations, national humiliations, and the Marshall Plan; a Paris at its lowest ebb, at its least glamorous. An insight that gave Paz strength and prevented him from repeating the Latin American admiration of French culture was that war-devastated Paris in 1945 did not differ from any other third-world

capital. In a footnote to *El Laberinto de la soledad* (1950) he wrote:
"When I arrived in France in 1945 I noted with amazement that
the fashion of the young of certain areas . . . reminded me of the
Pachucos of Southern California" (*L,* 13–16). What a relief that
these left-bank students and bohemians were just as lost and homeless as the *Pachucos!* The root perception behind *El laberinto de la
soledad:* the human condition was one behind the masks and idio-
syncracies of particular cultures.

This partially explains why Paz was not awed by Breton in 1945.
Another factor in Paz's favor derived from Breton's attitudes to
Mexico, one of his naturally surrealist countries. Mexico figured
overlarge in the surrealist map of the world (1929).[6] And Breton
visited Mexico in 1938 especially to talk and collaborate with Trotsky. Breton's short stay included perceptions of a dawn vision of a
woman-child in Guadalajara, the paintings of Frida Kahlo and Tamayo, Mexican landscape and its violent, excessive history, even
Mexican jumping beans (Breton broke with Roger Caillois over these
beans, refusing to crack one open to investigate the mystery that
made it jump).[7] Although Breton did not speak or read Spanish,
he was predisposed to accept Paz and indeed made Paz represent
mysterious Mexico, saying in 1956 that Paz conveyed a "gripping
image of Mexico," combining fervor, spiritual avidity, and revolutionary poetic ambitions. Earlier, in 1952, Breton had included
Paz within surrealist orthodoxy. Jean Louis Bédouin's anthology *La
poésie surréaliste* (1964) confirmed this by including Paz in translation.[8]

Paz dabbled with automatic writing but, like Xavier Villaurrutia
before him, soon rejected this discipline akin to meditation's emptying of the mind as too hard to achieve; basically, automatic writing
was a rough draft that needed to be worked into a text or a poem,
a view shared by Breton's practice as a poet (but not as a theoretician)
in the 1940s and 1950s. Paz signed a few collective manifestos and
accusations in 1951, contributed to some of the official magazines
like *Le surréalisme, même,* participated in some of the exhibitions,
and, despite his diplomatic post, engaged in protests like carrying
a placard defending Luis Buñuel's *Los olvidados* (The forgotten ones)
in the 1951 Cannes film festival. But Paz always felt that as a poet
writing in Spanish, he could not belong to the group. Only the
international language of painting allowed foreigners into the group,
only at this level was surrealism truly cosmopolitan.[9]

In 1967 Paz wrote that his activities in the group were "tangential" and this is true. Right from his first literary contact with some of the surrealist texts, especially Breton's *L'Amour fou* (Mad love) translated in *Sur* (1936), Paz had stressed not the techniques like automatic writing or games or chance associations or dream telling or trouvailles but surrealism's "intransigent affirmation of certain values" (*Pe*, 76). He sifted critically these values from the literary mannerisms that were bound to be imitated badly and turn into clichés. He lifted surrealism out of its time and historical/social contexts to make it an attitude of mind based on the subversive values of erotic love, the Other (woman), and inspiration.[10]

Because surrealism offered Paz a critical alternative to politics, nationalism, and ideologies—the spirit of the system—based on a "moral spirit" (*Pe*, 271) Paz defined it as a wisdom, a poetics resolving the dilemma of how to live poetically in a hostile Godless world (*Pu*, 280). Surrealism became Paz's "new sacred," affirming love liberty and poetry (*Pe*, 182). This new sacred makes sense if we fuse it with Paz's impasse of the 1940s. Surrealism became his "desperate attempt to find a way out" (*Pe*, 165), a phrase that sums up a period. By 1959 Paz told Couffon that surrealism had been crucial to him as a mentality; he had rescued the ideas of love and liberty.[11] Paz's absorption of surrealism emerged later in *El arco y la lira* (The bow and the Lyre, 1956), his passionate exploration of poetics.

In 1984 Paz penned a *mea culpa* accusing himself for not having appreciated Breton's moral position earlier, for Breton became disenchanted with Stalin in 1930 while only in 1951 in *Sur* did Paz publish a report on Stalin's concentration camps: (*S*, 110–11; *O*, 235–38). In 1958 Paz reviewed the Pasternak affair. He defended Pasternak's "individualist sensibility" and argued that politics, an abstract passion, dehumanizes man while love humanizes. Paz adopted this clarified moral stance from Breton. Love redeems man from the labyrinths of solitude of history: "In and through history each man can find himself and stop being an abstract entity who belongs to a social, ideological, or racial category and become again an unique, unrepeatable person" (*Pu*, 53). Surrealist love promised to restore man's inner life. Thus Paz labeled it the new sacred, the new *sagesse*.

Paz met and befriended the surrealist poet Benjamin Péret (1899–1959) in Spain in 1937. Péret, one of the closest and most faithful of Breton's original 1924 surrealist manifesto supporters, lived in Mexico (1941–48), contributed to Wolfgang Paalen's magazine *Dyn*, translated the Mayan classic *Livre de Chilam Balam de Chumayel* into French (1955) and Paz's *Piedra de sol* (1962).[12] Péret introduced Paz to Breton in the café of the Place Blanche in the late 1940s in Paris. But there are few traces of Péret's poetry in Paz's;[13] in 1959 Paz told Couffon that what he admired most in Péret was his "moral example."[14] In 1959 Paz attended Péret's funeral and published an uncollected obituary in *Les Lettres nouvelles* (1959) where he recalled their first meeting during one of the darkest periods of Western history (Péret fought under Durruti in the Spanish Civil War). Paz found Péret's attitudes to the horrors of twentieth-century history "uncorruptible," resisting all temptations to abdicate his opposition to authority. Thanks to Péret's faith in life, "the night of this century is not absolute."[15] He again met a still innocent Péret just before his death and cites Péret's poems *Je sublime* (1936) and *Air mexicain* (1952) as examples of this rebellious youthfulness. Paz approved of Péret's tract defending poetry as the only means of fighting social oppression in the name of freedom, its moment of publication (1945), and title *Le Déshonneur des poètes* (Poets' dishonor) acutely shared by both poets.[16] Paz especially admired Péret's alert mind, his spiritual "direction" that had always tried to reconcile life and poetry. Paz ended his note remembering vividly a moving encounter he had chatting with Péret and Breton in a café: "since then the universal night and my personal night have become clearer."[17] Paz's poem "Noche en claro" (Sleepless night), whose title acts as a metaphor for those dark ages and leads on to his later *Pasado en claro* (1975) evokes this emotive meeting in a café in Paris in 1959. It opens *Salamandra* (Salamander 1962) and is dedicated to both Péret and Breton. The poem sets its own realistic scene in the café de Inglaterra at 10:00 P.M., the three poets alone during a Parisian autumn. The strange sensation of some immanent revelation stimulated them: "Algo se prepara dijo uno entre nosotros" (Something is going to happen said one of us, *P*, 349). Paz then reverts to a revelation of life's horror that he had undergone in London's subway system:

> En lugar de ojos
>   abominación de espejos cegados
>   En lugar de labios
>   raya de borrosas costuras
> Nadie tenía sangre nadie tenía nombre
> no teníamos cuerpo ni espíritu

no teníamos cara
El tiempo daba vueltas y vueltas y no pasaba
no pasaba nada sino el tiempo que pasa y regresa y no pasa.
(*P*, 350)

(Instead of eyes / abomination of blind mirrors / Instead of lips / a scratch of blurred seams / Nobody had blood nobody had a name / we didn't have a body or a mind / we didn't have a face / time turned round and round and didn't pass / nothing happened except time that passed, returned and didn't pass.)

Then lovers appeared and the surrealist force of love in this underworld hell made itself visible, tattooed on the girl's fingers (in the poem a drawing of a hand with *LOVE* spelled on each finger): "mano que das el sueño y das la resurrección" (hand that gives the dream and gives resurrection, *P*, 351). The clear surrealist values are opposed to the night. In the poem the three poets then split up but "mis amigos se alejan / llevo sus palabras como un tesoro ardiendo" (my friends leave / but I take their words like a burning treasure, *P*, 352). Paz's debt to Péret and Breton becomes transparent; surrealism was Paz's treasure in the foul cold war days of the twentieth century: "siglo tallado en un aullido / pirámide de sangre" (century shaped in a howl / pyramid of blood, *P*, 352). The poem ends with an elegy of the City, Woman, and presence as alternatives to this history, "el lugar de la cita" (the place of the appointment) where this *cita* was with Péret and Breton and a woman and with poetry.

Paz owes André Breton even more as his moral example. "Noche en claro," where the café meeting clarified the night of history, suggests Paz's liberating relationship with a father figure. His obituary on Breton (first appearing in the *Nouvelle Revue française* in 1967) can be read as one of his most typical prose essays written in a jumbled, repetitive, circular language fusing enthusiasm with acute insights. Its rhythms and long sentences should be savored in their entirety. It is here that Paz confesses that Breton for him was far more than a great poet; "a man of honor," a "religious" man whose beliefs about innocence and love were based on "an act of faith" (*C*, 53). Breton's ambition was not to create a poetic school but a "movement of total liberation" (*C*, 53). Paz singled out "magnetism" as the most succinct word to characterize both Breton's views on language and poetry and his personality (*magnetism* is a word that Paz also often employs).

In this obituary Paz refers to his personal relationship to Breton. First he confesses his fear of Breton's moral authority: "I confess that for a long time the idea of doing or saying something that might provoke his reprobation kept me awake" (*C*, 57). Paz then internalized this fear: "I will say that many times when I write it is as if I held a silent dialogue with Breton: retort, answer, coincidence, divergence, homage, all at once" (*C*, 58). Paz remained loyal to Breton's basic belief in love: "I have tried to be faithful to this revelation; the word *love* keeps all its powers intact for me" (*C*, 59).

In his friendship over the years Paz singled out one meeting in 1964 in Les Halles in Paris (he promised to tell the story in full but has not yet) that marked Paz and concerned a dialogue about the future of surrealism. Paz had called it the sacred disease of the West (he repeated this to Carlos Monsiváis in 1967)[18] while Breton disagreed, feeling that surrealism had to go underground and separate itself from the dire present moment. To Breton Paz reaffirmed his belief that surrealism would never die out, its spiritual rebellion "would live on the margins, would be the *other* voice" (*C*, 60). Surrealism became Paz's longed-for alternative to political revolution.

Perhaps Paz's most telling confession concerns Breton's contacting life outside the limits of successive time and the nightmare of history, and hinting at Paz's notion of the liberating epiphanic *instante:* "Breton several times broke that prison, he extended or negated time, and for a measureless instant, coincided with the other time. This experience, nucleus of his life and thought, is invulnerable and untouchable. Knowing this reconciles me to his death and to all dying" (*C*, 64). "To all dying" could encapsulate surrealism's breadth. And isn't this a resolution of alienation from dehumanizing history? What Breton confirmed in the Paz of the late 1940s was a faith in the values of poetry to cope with death by generating within the poem, communally for readers, an experience of the other time.

In 1973 Paz published an irate letter to Fernando Gamboa, organizer of an exhibition on surrealism in Mexico City. Paz defended André Breton because the exhibition catalog had amputated surrealism from its subversive revulsion for capitalism, Christianity, and the monstrous perversion of Russian socialism. Paz resented the denigrating view of Breton's lucidity faced with Stalin in the 1930s.[19] He highlighted the postwar years as those where the surrealists became "one of the very few centers of opposition to the hegemonic

propaganda of both powers" (*I*, 151). And those were the days when
Paz participated in the Parisian group.

Still, in 1974 Paz continued to define surrealism along ethical
lines: "Surrealism was not an aesthetic or a school or a manner: it
was a total, vital attitude—both ethical and aesthetic—that expressed itself in action and participation" (*I*, 156). This emphasis
on action is where Paz fused his previous revolutionary beliefs with
Bretonian postwar surrealism.

In *Vuelta* (1976) Paz collected a poem that had been painted along
a spiral gallery leading into the 1973 surrealist exhibition. Surrealism was not inside this gallery, but outside, alive, in the air,
mixed with life's marvelous properties: "It is within one's reach /
it is the moment when man / *is*" (*P*, 622). Paz's "is" suggests
surrealism's confusion with essence, desires, roots, otherness, truth.
To summarize Paz's relationship with Breton: he defined Breton (to
Julio Scherer) as one of the few "hombres de conciencia" (men of
consciousness) in the twentieth century (*O*, 329).

In 1959, in a foreword to Blanca Varela's poems, Paz invoked
the atmosphere of his surrealist days in postwar, cold-war Paris; it
was like living in a tunnel without an exit. A long uniform wall
imprisoned people: a hopeless, aimless alienation. But not everybody
was resigned to this hell: some turned to philosophy or politics (like
Sartre), others (the surrealists) sought a *salida* (a way out) inside
themselves. Small groups of despairing people formed in cafés:
"Nothing united us, except our search, our tedium, despair, desire"
(*Pu*, 117). He names the café where they listened to jazz, drank
rum, danced, and heard poems by Michaux and Artaud read aloud.
The Latin Americans especially suffered the grey Parisian hopeless-
ness, dreaming of their volcanoes, suns, and adobe villages. Paz
gives the Christian names of some of his cosmopolitan companions:
Kostos (Papaioannou, remembered by Paz when he died in *Hombres
en su siglo*, 1984), Rufino (Tamayo), Elena (Garro), Benjamin (Péret),
André and Elisa (Breton), Jean-Clarence (Lambert, Paz's principal
translator into French). Last, Paz defined their view of art as exorcisms (cf. Henri Michaux's *Exorcismes*, 1943) against the noise,
yawns, sirens, and bombs. Paz: "To write was to defend ourselves,
to defend life. Poetry was an act of self-defence" (*Pu*, 117). For life
had been cheapened by the war, the gulags, and the concentration
camps, and Paz and his companions insisted on defending this life,
exorcizing the devils of history. It was Breton who employed the

term self-defense for poetry in 1926 and again in a poem "Sur la route de San Romano" (1948; translated by Paz into Spanish in *Versiones y diversiones*, 1974) where "L'étreinte poétique comme l'étreinte de chair / tant qu'elle dure / *défend* toute echappée sur la misère du monde" (my italics; The poetic embrace, like the flesh embrace / as long as it lasts / forbids all fall into the world's misery).[20]

Art became a spell cast against an opaque, fallen world. When Paz defined Blanca Varela's poems, he equated "surrealist poet" (not a manner of writing but a spiritual lineage) with "true" poet. Paz's stance toward the ruins of the European war was: no more utopias (revolutionary politics), no more imaginary worlds (escapist art), but a naming and redeeming of reality through the inner transformation of the poet himself: "a change of being of the poet himself" (*Pu*, 121). Poetry expresses "a conscience that awakens," a critical phrase that implies a getting to know the enemy and lucidity and consciousness. The poet awakens to the world as it is beyond its ruins, his transformation to do with inner consciousness explored in language.

The poems written during those years in the tunnel and published in *Libertad bajo palabra* (1949) must be read as conscious exorcisms. "El prisionero," dated 1948 and a fundamental philosophical poem, combines the prisoner the marquis de Sade (actually in prison most of his life and a prisoner of his selfish rational philosophy) with contemporary rational man, creator of Sadean war technology. Paz grounds the poem in a powerful image of transparent rigidity: "Prisionero en tu castillo de cristal de roca" (prisoner in your castle of rock crystal, *P*, 121) that echoes Breton and the cold beauty of de Sade's technique of suppressing others to become insensible to passions and life.[21] This poem veers from surrealist orthodoxy—de Sade as hero, as mentor of revolt—to correct Breton's mistaken admiration for such an inhuman person—described in the poem as a mask, an iceberg, and a torture instrument, and associated with elephant's reasoning, atrocities, broken-down clockwork, etc. Paz redefines Breton's true tradition (Rousseau, nature, passionate love, woman) against de Sade. In the 1940s, to Paz a Latin American, de Sade had become the monster of European rationalism. Against this, love is the only answer to de Sade's self-mirror of emptiness. Paz again calls up the whole period in Europe, the despair of recuperating life and a community negated by the likes of de Sade. Paz's answer: "Solo en mi semejante me trasciendo" (only in my fellow can I transcend myself, *P*, 122). Love of the other (woman) transcends the solitary self to create a fragile alternative reality (lovers coupling) that foretells a society based on this kind of relationship. The poem was written in Avignon, near the ruins of de Sade's castle. "En la calzada" (On the highway), dated Paris 1946, offers an alternative reality to that of Paris (the tunnel of the 1940s). The poem follows Michaux's black-humored substitution of so-called reality for one based on fantasy. It builds up in a way typical of the Paz of the years 1945–58: from a setting in a conventional reality to an inner, passionate mental space compacted into overlapping images, analogies, and similes in long sinuous lines that refuse to be read slowly, a sort of orchestral submersion in a "leafy paradise."

The grounding reality is an avenue of chestnut trees in leaf, moved by the wind; the poem then transcends this avenue to rediscover true nature: "un baile antiguo"`(an ancient dance, *P,* 118). As the poet penetrates this green submarine avenue to a magical land— "eterna la hoja verde, / el agua siempre niña" (the green leaf eternal, / the water always a young girl, *P,* 118)—the word *always* occurs seven times in four lines and reveals the transposition from the temporal world of sordid history to the permanent, eternal one within each person. The poet wants to seize a young girl passerby, ignorant of this other reality, and plant her among the chestnuts, water her, watch her grow, touch her, speak to her, rest with her, and fall erotically into her: the word *green* suggests the erotic world of the poet's imagination transforming reality. The last controlling verb is *caer* (to fall):

> caer en gotas anchas,
> gotas de fuego,
> gotas de sangre al rojo blanco,
> como cae la semilla cuando estalla la espiga en el aire,
> como cae la estrella en la honda matriz de la noche,
> como cae el avión en llamas y el bosque se incendia.
>
> (*L,* 107)

(to fall in wide drops / drops of fire, / drops of blood white-hot, / like the seed falls when the ear of grain bursts in the air, / like the star falls into the deep matrix of the night, / like the plane falls in flames and the wood catches fire.)

Reading these lines, almost pantingly, mimics the crescendo of love, or its vertigo, its fall. All the natural analogies—fire, water, blood,

seed, wheat, air, night, star—are shattered by the last surprising
line (an echo of a Péret poem "Je sublime")[22] where the fire (of
imagination, of passion) burns and purges the lovers, allowing them
to be reborn Phoenix-like out of the tunnel of twentieth-century
life. In 1979 Paz excised this ending, leaving the poem less desperate, less hectic.

Equally exalting of the other, imaginary reality is Paz's lovely
"Más allá del amor" (Beyond love), first published in 1948. It
employs the same imagery as Paz's prose on Blanca Varela to convey
the hollow reality of the 1940s in Paris. The opening line encap-
sulates the threat on the poet's inner harmony: "Todo nos amenaza"
(everything threatens us, *P*, 131); the rest of the poem lists the
enemies:

el tiempo, que en vivientes fragmentos divide
al que fui
          del que seré,
como el machete a la culebra;
la conciencia, la transparencia traspasada,
la mirada ciega de mirarse mirar;
las palabras, guantes grises, polvo mental sobre la yerba, el agua, la piel;
nuestros nombres, que entre tú y yo se levantan
murallas de vacío que ninguna trompeta derrumba.

                                                        (*P*, 131)

(time that divides into living fragments / I who was / from I who will
be, / like the machete with the snake; / conscience, transparency pierced, /
the blind look of looking at oneself looking; / words, grey gloves, mental
dust on the grass, water, skin; / our names that between you and I rise
up / walls of emptiness that no trumpet tumbles down.)

The enemy is successive time or history—and Paz uses a Mexican
simile to convey time's violence on the individual—as well as the
blind look (surely a reference to Sartre's "regard"), the political
philosophy that negates inner life and the dead words of all those
in power, dust on the beauty of nature; the enemy lies within as
the lack of recognition of the other. The poem then posits the life
that demands to be redeemed; it cannot be found in dreams, not
in madness, not even in love:

                        más allá de nosotros,

en las fronteras del ser y el estar,
una vida más vida nos reclama.
(*P*, 131)

(Beyond us, / in the frontiers of being, / a life more life reclaims us.)

The postwar depressive mood urges the Mexican poet to find a life beyond what has passed for life, beyond all that is given. The poem ends exhorting the "you" to submit to the night's expansion of possibilities and prepare for an experience that surpasses what passes for love; again Paz threads a link of archetypal analogies—star, bread, cup—to convey the ecstasy of being at the borders between clock and social time and "eternity," for man is, and it is the last line: "pausa de sangre entre este tiempo y otro sin medida" (a pause of blood between this time and the other without measure, *P*, 132). The poem fulfills its ambition by founding a language of consciousness (not to be confused with rationality or common sense) on to ecstasy. In this sense, Paz cannot be called a mystic, for he tries to put a name or an image or an analogy to the experience of relief from history. No mindless sensations, but a *conciencia* (conscience, a moral awareness) of man's potential to change.

Paz exalts woman as the other, man's only salvation in such grim days (and woman is both a concrete entity outside the poem and an energy released by the poem). Salvation through the other, the theme of "El prisionero," is elaborated in "Cuerpo a la vista" (Body in view), a title that suggests Jorge Guillén's "Más allá" or "Desnudo," poems much admired and later commented on by Paz,[23] with the same eulogy of the woman's naked body. But Paz offsets Guillén's enthusiastic but controlled stanzas with long lines, dense overlapping analogies and a crescendo of images reaching a hectic end similar to "En la calzada." Woman's body, then, reveals itself to the poet's glance as a promise of transformation: her hair, mouth, skin, valleys, creeks, plateaus become his erotic geography, his world. The poem offers surprising images: "Tus ojos son los ojos fijos del tigre / y un minuto después son los ojos húmedos del perro" (your eyes are the fixed eyes of the tiger / and a minute later the humid eyes of a dog, *P*, 126), where "her" eyes change like her moods and identities; or: "Siempre hay abejas en tu pelo" (there are always bees in your hair, *P*, 126), a stunning line—that first alerted Julio Cortázar to Paz in a review in *Sur* in 1949[24]—that fuses golden

44   OCTAVIO PAZ

hair with honey, bees, sticky sweetness, movement, and even dan-
ger. This cosmic woman's sexuality focuses the poet's cascade of
analogies. It is as if the poet avoids an anatomical description because
it is woman who releases his capacity to be a poet and fix in words
both his ecstasy and his consciousness of this exalted state.
   The ending of the poem is at once strangely explicit, wonderfully
erotic, and clearly metaphysical:

   Entre tus piernas hay un pozo de agua dormida,
   bahía donde el mar de noche se aquieta, negro caballo de espuma,
   cueva al pie de la montaña que esconde un tesoro,
   boca del horno donde se hacen las hostias,
   sonrientes labios entreabiertos y atroces,
   nupcias de la luz y la sombra, de lo visible y lo invisible
   (allí espera la carne su resurrección y el día de la vida perdurable).
                                                    (P, 126–27)

(Between your legs there is a well of dormant water, / bay where the sea
at night quietens down, black horse of foam, / cave at the foot of a mountain
that hides a treasure, / oven mouth that makes hosts / smiling lips half
open and atrocious / nuptials of light and shade, visibility and invisibility /
[there flesh awaits its resurrection and the day of life everlasting].)

This expansion of "vagina" into well, bay, cave, and mouth functions
in terms of that everlasting life that only lovers taste and where
opposites are united, André Breton's still point, denied as a value
in the twilight world of the twentieth century.[25] The poem echoes
César Vallejo's *Trilce* poem "XIII" ("Pienso en tu sexo . . ."—
I think of your sex)[26] in its explicitness and Ramón López Velarde's
"Hormigas" (Ants) of *Zozobra* (Anxiety), which links mouth/oven/
hosts in terms of woman's mouth, in its sensuality.[27] But the movement of the poem is very Pazian. It ends:

   Patria de sangre,
   única tierra que conozco y me conoce,
   única patria en la que creo,
   única puerta al infinito.
                                                    (P, 127)

(Motherhood of blood, / only land which I know and knows me, / only
motherland in which I believe, / only door to the infinite.)

Here is Paz's new erotic credo: he switches allegiances from Mexico and catholicism to the "patria/tierra" of woman, his double and opposite with whom love becomes his salvation, the only experience that grants him an identity beyond history, politics, ideology, materialism, and bureaucracy; the contrary to his age's tunnel or labyrinth was the infinite gained through love. It is in this sense that love is a subversive activity because it is Paz's alternative to revolutionary politics.

Hymn among the Ruins

The closing poem of *Libertad bajo palabra* (1949), "Himno entre ruinas (Hymn among the ruins, one of Paz's densest, most interpreted poems) also opens *La estación violenta* (The violent season) of 1958. This crucial poem sets out to describe the poet's alienation in the 1940s and to resolve this by restoring innocence, sensuality, and life with a consciousness of what a mere poem can do to integrate the divided poet (and reader). And it tries to achieve this ambitious end lyrically.

It is dated Naples, 1948, with an epigraph that sets the scene historically and geographically with a quotation from Góngora's *Fábula de Polifemo y Galatea* (Fable of Polyphemus and Galatea, 1613)—Polyphemus, the envious Cyclops, appears in the poem. The physical landscape of Sicily, with its abundant, fertile nature, enters Paz's poem from Góngora, as does the notion of the uncorrupt world of poetry, opposed to the mindless violence of World War II, the rivalry between Galatea and Polifemo modernized. The title of the poem combines the need for a hymn (a sacralizing poem) to redeem the ruined world of the 1940s; the ruins are those of classical antiquity, Europe after the war, Mexico after the revolution, dead language itself, with echoes of T. S. Eliot's *The Waste Land*. The poet quite literally builds up his poem from fragments that he has unearthed, an archeological analogy natural for a Mexican. The poem is severely structured like a pyramid with six stanzas alternating lowercase with italics (perhaps for two voices) and contrasting sunlight with night as metaphorical value systems, ending with a synthesis, the seventh magical-biblical stanza capping the pyramid, explicitly stating in a nonlyric, philosophical discourse, what Paz intended—or hoped—poetry could do for divided twentieth-century man.

The opening stanza suggests the origin of the world—the primal egg, the sun, exposing the perfect appearances of the island in a moment of time. Behind the first eleven lines is an elaborate metaphor of the rising sun, its rays the feathers of a hen whose dawn cry (cock and hen confused) is impartial and beneficial to all life. This sun hen lays its golden egg that spills its light over the sea. This world without modern man is a paradise: "Las apariencias son hermosas en esta su verdad momentánea" (appearances are beautiful in this their momentary truth, P, 233). And this beauty is divine: "Todo es dios" (all is god, P, 233).

God is simply light, while man in this century is a "muerto en vida" (a living dead, P, 233). Our gloss on Paz's rich, suggestive, and controlled imagery would be: the world itself did not fabricate the "tunnel" of the 1940s: man has been his own undoing. A return to this primal world would be salutary, a reminder of a lost harmony, of an original participation (Paz's borrowing from Lévy-Bruhl's primitive's participation).

The second stanza in italics opposes night to this metaphorical sun and captures the Mexican experience of universal alienation, the matter of *El laberinto de la soledad*, condensed into a few lines:

> *Cae la noche sobre Teotihuacán.*
> *En lo alto de la pirámide los muchachos fuman marihuana,*
> *suenan guitarras roncas.*
>
> (P, 233)

(Night falls on Teotihuacán. / On the top of the pyramid boys smoke marihuana, / harsh guitars sound.)

The Mexican is split from a shared meaningful past. The Aztec pyramid becomes a place to smoke dope and play tuneless music. Opposed to the postrevolutionary politicized tradition Paz reveals the Mexican's homelessness as a twentieth-century drama: "¿Qué yerba, qué agua de vida ha de darnos la vida . . . ?" (what herb, what life water can give us life?, P, 233). Clearly not marihuana. Paz seeks that fuller life experienced in Spain that has been betrayed by the war and by history. The poet asks, parodying the archeologist: "dónde desenterrar la palabra" (where to unearth the word, P, 233), a word that would grant the consciousness that would root man back to life. Paz's vision of Mexico underlines the lack of harmony: "El canto mexicano estalla en un carajo" (the Mexican song bursts into a curse, *P*, 234). The violence of the *carajo* (the Revolution?), studied excitingly in *El laberinto de la soledad*, severs the Mexican from contact with his roots: "piedra que nos cierra las puertas del contacto" (stone that blocks the door of contact, *P*, 234). No privileges, the Mexican suffers the Western disease of history.

The third stanza returns to the sun-drenched sensual world that can teach urban man something vital. The poet's ideas are marvelously embodied in the actual lines. The world caught through the senses liberated from history is immediate, irrefutable: "Los ojos ven, las manos tocan" (eyes see, hands touch, *P*, 234). The poet's vision of the simple life discards all that alienates man from the innocence of touch: "Bastan aquí unas cuantas cosas" (only a few things are needed here, *P*, 234). This is his reaction to the evils of technology resulting in the atom bomb of 1945. In the late 1930s Paz wrote the poem "La vida sencilla" (The simple life) which opens "Llamar al pan el pan y que aparezca / sobre el mantel el pan de cada día" (to call bread bread and that it appears / this every day bread on the tablecloth, *P*, 90). In the 1930s the poet had only to pronounce the basic verities, like bread is the staff of life, and the word lost its contaminated associations to become bread again; thus the poet could "seize life." The idea of recovering the elemental necessities of life in order to enjoy living was what Paz eagerly appreciated during the Spanish Civil War, and later in ration-book Europe.

The Spanish poet Juan Gil-Albert, Paz's secretary on *Taller*, recalled that surviving in the euphoria of the Spanish Civil War, amid the camaraderie and breakdown of alientating social hierarchies, lead to a "brusque rebirth of the primary appetites" where fundamental instincts, suppressed in the complexities of urban cultured life, became exciting discoveries.[28] Spain revealed to Paz his most ancient roots, as an inner buried innocence. This innocence is simply the instinctual, animal life. During an air raid in Valencia Paz shared food with some peasants cowering in a vineyard: "eating (bread, a melon, cheese, wine) with those peasants during a bombardment . . . that's something I can't forget."[29] These peasants taught Paz the elemental values of companionship (cf. *pan*). He re-created this meal in this poem:

tuna, espinoso planeta coral,
higos encapuchados,
uvas con gusto a resurrección,
almejas, virginidades ariscas,
sal, queso, vino, pan solar.
(P, 234)

(Prickly pear, thorny coral planet, / hooded figs, / grapes with a taste of
resurrection, / clams, shy virginities, / salt, cheese, wine, solar bread.)

The result of this simple life is a poet who learns to readapt to
the world. The stanza ends on a rich image: "La luz crea templos
en el mar" (Light creates temples on the sea, P, 234). Nature is
sacralized by shafts of light, a cathedral with pillars of light.

The fourth stanza (the second in italics) establishes the twentieth
century with its anemic sun (the cold Parisian sun, the bloodless
sun of urban civilizations). Paz stretches the disease of alienation to
cover the Western world, locked in its sterile cold war: "Nueva York,
Londres, Moscú. / La sombra cubre el llano con su yedra fantasma" (New
York, London, Moscow. / The shadow covers the plain with its fantasmal
ivy, P, 234). Man has shrunk to a T. S. Eliot rat (The Hollow Men),
a city sheep (docile crowds), a domesticated biped fed to the rich
(capitalism's voracity). This shadow is the dehumanized life under
omnipotent states, both communist and capitalist (O, 9).

The fifth stanza returns dialectically to what the poet learned
from the natural world and opens with an echo of the third: "Ver,
tocar formas hermosas, diarias" (To see, to touch beautiful daily
forms, P, 234). Dead symbols like wine become alive. Then the
poet appears with a magnificent simile that condenses the whole
enterprise into one image: "Como el coral sus ramas en el agua /
extiendo mis sentidos en la hora viva" (like the coral's branches in
the water / I extend my senses in the living hour P, 234). The
richness of recovered life is like a lagoon with man a coral reaching
out in every imaginable direction. The poet, his innocent senses
liberated, discovers a hora viva in the ruins of the European war.
The poem is both a hymn of hope and a lesson.

The stanza ends with an exclamation mark, an ecstasy of contact
like a rebirth: "¡Oh mediodía, espiga henchida de minutos, / copa
de eternidad!" (oh midday, ear of corn swollen with minutes / cup
of eternity!, P, 235). This fragile recovery of true life during a
momentary ecstasy is suggested in a metaphor of the sun leaving

no shadows. But this is a mental illumination, conveyed in ancient, biblical symbols *(espiga, copa)*, for it is an intellectual insight. But the poem does not end here. The sixth italicized stanza shifts the ruined world from Mexico, New York, London, and Moscow to how these infested places are internalized in the poet as systems, as mentalities. T. S. Eliot's waste land is both London and his mind. Here the poet's thoughts become a labyrinth where the flow-river of thought finds no outlet. The poet's anguish of being stuck in a tunnel in a hopeless world: "¿Y todo ha de parar en este chapoteo de aguas muertas?" (and will everything have to stop in this splashing of dead waters?, *P*, 235).

The poem immediately answers the question in its seventh, crowning stanza with a No! so important that Paz does not confide in images or a lyrical approach: he interprets this experience for the reader: "¡Día, redondo día, / luminosa naranja de veinticuatro gajos, / todos atravesados por una misma y amarilla dulzura!" (Day, round day, / luminous orange of twenty-four segments, / all crossed with an identical yellow sweetness, *P*, 235). A potentially stunning resolution of the simple life (orange groves abound in the Mediterranean), uniting sun, health, taste, and resolving alienation. But the image is flawed by the twenty-four segments, the clock/sun/fruit. This suggests an orange of sweet, real sensual time as the forbidden fruit that man must eat—orange more appropriate than the Northern apple for Paz, who, in an earlier poem has, "es morder la naranja prohibida" (it is to bite the forbidden orange, *P*, 80). The poet's solution becomes an intellectual poem dealing with qualities of consciousness; it is being aware and lucid that count. Paz: "La inteligencia al fin encarna, / se reconcilian las dos mitades enemigas / y la conciencia-espejo se licúa," (intelligence at last embodies / the two enemy halves are reconciled / and the conscience mirror turns liquid, *P*, 235). Arid, waste land, rational intelligence, is linked back to the body, no more duality, no body-mind split. Man's reason fuses with his innocent senses and he experiences integration as a heightened consciousness. The mirror-self (guilt and self-centeredness) flows back into real time. Are these lines too explicit, too abstract for the poem? Or has the poem led up to this perception? The problem qualifies all Paz's poetry, for he dismisses lyrical obscurity to seek intellectual lucidity (*luz*, light, the central motif of the poem). The poem must be explicit in order to dispense its wisdom and teach how to escape the tunnel of the 1940s.

The poem ends with easily interpretable images of alienation vanquished: "vuelve a ser fuente, manantial de fábulas: / Hombre, árbol de imágenes, / palabras que son flores que son frutos que son actos" (returns to being a spring, source of fables: / Man, tree of images, / words that are flowers that are fruit that are acts, *P, 235*). The lesson is available to all men; its universality joins all the world into one community, not Mexican, Russian, or French. Rooting yourself back like a tree to the natural world releases a natural language that flows up like sap. This is the original, metaphorical language of images spoken once when all men were poets. The poet's natural words would rise up like flowers or fruit and change our lives by focusing our awareness on the evils of the twentieth century. Only this kind of lucid poetry can make us act to change ourselves, then others and society. This is a deeper politics than his 1930s position; it is a socialism buried in the innocence of the senses. The surrealist poets in the 1940s sought to change man first, then perhaps change the world: the surrealist revolution.

According to Paz (to Ríos, 1971) this poem implies voices (the enemies or others) inside each person and is scored to be read by four different voices, a dialogue with the world in oneself. He told Carballo (1958) that the ruins of the past and present and the ruins in each individual's mind can be transformed by discovering how to be a poet, and this meant not scribbling verse but locating "eternity" inside himself and giving a name (that is, an awareness) to what otherwise might be fleeting sensations.[30] This ethical drive motivates the poem.

The Labyrinth of Solitude

Being a Mexican in Paris during those years sharpened Paz's sense of national identity, helping him sift the accidental from the mythic, the false and political from the essence. His passionate study of *mexicanidad,* the dilemmas of being a Mexican in the twentieth century, called *El laberinto de la soledad* (1950), a title evoking existential terms, can be read on several levels, but primarily as the veiled autobiography of a poet looking on to his national experience from Paris, with nostalgia and exasperation. That this book has been read as an objective account of Mexican psychology and history, an intelligent tourist's guide, and that this work continues a tradition embodied by Ortega y Gasset and Samuel Ramos that has profoundly influenced many Mexicans (Carlos Fuentes, Juan Rulfo), will be taken for granted.[31] *El laberinto de la soledad*'s most vivid meanings emerge as the work of a poet exploring the absence of a meaningful life, a defense of poetry and its values. Paz modestly proposed: "I do not claim to do anything but clarify for myself the sense of certain experiences and I admit that perhaps its only value is as a personal answer to a personal question" (*L*, 60). But this personal question remains hidden as if the book itself embodies Paz's view of the reticent, closed Mexican male. Paz deliberately universalized his experiences in keeping with his basic insight that the homeless, alienated predicament of the twentieth-century Mexican is shared by all in Western culture.

The book began as essays written in Paris and published in Mexico in *Cuadernos americanos;* they appeared in book form in 1950, and a second enlarged edition in 1959 added a vital appendix entitled "The Dialectic of Solitude" in which Paz enunciates his principles. This appendix should be read as a preface in order to evaluate the chapters on the Mexican, his masks, the women, attitudes to death, sex, religion, and so on.

Two basic insights (already mentioned) govern the book. The first is Paz's vision of the New Man in Spain during the Civil War, a true socialist society of poets with everybody turned poet and become free. It is a vision that resolved all forms of alienation. The second is Paz's awareness that the Californian Pachuco, stripped of all his cultural and national identities, did not differ from the left-bank Parisian: that this homelessness was endemic to Western man. Both insights exorcise propositions: that socialism is a utopian pipe-dream and that Mexicans are radically different and special. Undermining these became a relief, harboring a conviction. Paz said to Claude Fell (1975): "Moral criticism is self-revelation of what we hide, and as Freud taught, a relative . . . cure. In this sense my book wanted to be moral criticism" (*O*, 20).

In 1959 a hostile critic accused Paz of using his own concept of *ningunear* (to pretend someone is not there) to ignore enormous debts to Samuel Ramos's *El perfil del hombre y de la cultura en Mexico* (The profile of man and culture in Mexico, 1934).[32] Paz answered this jibe with a description of his intentions. Ramos wrote a pyschological account of the Mexican's inferiority complex, derived from Alfred Adler and Otto Rank, with Mexican history as motivated by this complex and a birth trauma. Ramos also referred to the

mask theory of identity and studied the *pelado,* especially his phall-
ically charged language. Paz accepted that Ramos was his starting
point; *El laberinto de la soledad* explored areas missed by Ramos. Paz
continued: "Ramos analysed an isolated type and omitted an historical examination, life as relationships . . . our myths . . . he
does not touch Mexican history or the Mexicans's vital relationship
with certain universal ideologies. Finally, he is not interested in
situating us in the world nor pointing out that Mexican life, above
all from the Revolution, and precisely because our Revolution is a
fragment of a wave of twentieth-century revolutions that flow into
universal history."[33] Paz substituted Ramos's psychology with history, with man as the place where history and poetry wage an
oscillating, continuous war. Paz's prime concern was not with economic change but with a spiritual revolution, with Camus's rebel
as model. Writing from Paris, Paz identified the enemies of man's
potential freedom as certain words made meaningless by industrial
society—"art, poetry, imagination, games, love, soul, dream, analogy"—to end that man's only remaining conquest is of inner not
outer space.[34] This surrealist critique opposes the Marxist view of
man as *homo economicus.* Paz's book is rooted in that moment in Paris
(1948; the polemic between Breton and Sartre; the discussion about
political engagement between Sartre and Camus) where this dialogue
(surrealism vs. Marxism) was at its bitterest.[35] Thus *El laberinto de
la soledad* describes how entrapped the Mexican is in his uncon-
sciously created prison and asks whether he (or anybody) can free
himself or if there is a way out of the labyrinth of history that has
severed man from himself and from the others that he needs in order
fully to be. This is Paz's variant of the topic in the Paris of the late
1940s.

　　Paz's premise links the Mexican's problem to all men's: "our
situation of alienation is that of the majority of people" (*L,* 159).
Mexicans discovered this revelation collectively (the idea that we as
individuals embody the clash between history and poetry abolishes
the differences between the individual and the collectivity) during
the Mexican Revolution (1910–17) where Mexico jettisoned its alien
masks. Only then did Mexico encounter its solitude, its nakedness,
its living for the day, its being orphaned from the past: overlapping
existentialist notions of authenticity, what is freedom, the mask,
the orphan, blocked communication with the other, etc., impres-
sionistically derived from Nietzsche, Heidegger, and Sartre. Paz

does not question these notions; they underscore his study as facts. But he modifies the pessimistic existential view with a surrealist "truth": all societies limit and deform man's desire, his potential for freedom, and only poetry reconciles man with true life. These surrealist notions also underscore the book and are never questioned. From values they become facts. Part of the book's exciting confusions flow from Paz's dependence on these "myths" to create his moral criticism.

Paz illustrates Mexico as a specific example of universal solitude through the first four chapters, concentrating on the *Pachuco* whose identity has shrunk to a self-humiliation expressed in loud clothes and foul language, attracting attention to himself because he has forsaken his heritage: language, religion, customs, beliefs. Paz contrasts the *Gringo* and the Mexican; he anatomizes the cult of machismo: the stoic, closed, silent Mexican man who does not dare be himself. Paz views Mexican woman—*la sufrida, la chingada* (the suffered one, the violated one)—as reflections of machismo. Woman is either whore or idol but "never herself" (*L,* 31). The most vivid sections expose the Mexican fascination with death and indifference to life, the peculiarly Mexican fiestas, the abuse of the swearword *chingar,* the only poetry left to Mexicans. Paz does not write clinically or objectively like a sociologist. His contorted syntax shifts and contradicts itself in a style analogous with the onrush of passion. In all, his summary of the Mexican makes depressing reading: he is alone, masked, fearful, distrusts others, is self-deceived, formal, living a constant lie. Paz: "All Mexican history . . . can be seen as a search for ourselves, deformed or masked by foreign institutions and of a form that expresses us" (*L,* 137). So Paz posits the desperate need for a *ruptura* as the culmination of the Mexican's alienating history.

The last four chapters form an alternative unity to constitute Paz's illuminatingly critical review of Mexican history, but not as a historian. He structures his view of history on the belief-experience that human nature is not entirely historical (art, love, games, ceremonies escape historical definition), though the historical part actively represses this other poetic side. Paz views history morally. A depth experience ruptures and modifies the surface flow of chronological history and refutes its dominance. But Paz never explains his premise; he believes in it as part of his war with Marxism; it generates his chain of analogies and metaphors.

Paz outlines his Joycean, moral view of history as atrociously real as a nightmare (Joyce: "History is a nightmare from which I am trying to awake")[36] where man's greatness lies in making beautiful, durable works out of the real substance of this nightmare. Paz calls this "transfiguring the nightmare into a vision, liberating ourselves, if only for an instant, from this deforming reality by means of creation" (L, 87). Paz's refusal to be subjugated by the nightmare (the fall of Spain, World War II, Stalin) raises the poet to the rank of hero, conscious of how to free himself through creativity. Only by reacting against history's real substance can man gain freedom. The experiential instant of liberation (and inevitable fall back into history) suggests a *ser* (a state of being) outside history, without ever defining this term. This potential state of liberation, *ser*, is granted to Mexico as if it were an individual.[37] So Mexican history becomes a dialectic (or rhythm) of solitude and communion, the ebb and flow of liberation/imprisonment, the *instante* and empty sequential time. Paz categorizes Mexican history in terms of its point in this continually oscillating rhythm. For example, after the Conquest imposed its alien order on Mexico, Catholicism created an open (i.e., liberating) system. But this state could not last and degenerated into a static society, a petrified, passive reflection of Spain (i.e., imprisoned in its labyrinth of solitude again). The nineteenth century attempts to substitute one form for another (liberalism, positivism), but only when the Revolution irrupts does Mexico's true face emerge, its roots discovered. Paz's Mexican Revolution becomes a "true revelation of our being" (L, 122), but the 1917 Constitution, the formation of the P.R.I. (Partido Revolucionario Institucional, the monolithic party that has been in power since founded by Calles in 1929) etc., soon deformed this spontaneous "communion" or liberation. Paz blamed politicians and those in power for using words to hide and oppress Mexico's true being. But what is this *ser?* Partly it is the buried indigenous past that emerges spontaneously, without a codified ideology; partly it's a return to the origins, *a la madre* (to the mother) and partly its an "explosion of reality" where Mexico has dared be itself. For any historian these are fuzzy, meaningless terms; yet within Paz's own submerged moral scale they are clear if not definable, for they refer to that experience of freedom, tasted in Spain, however momentary, that becomes Paz's only way of defining man.

Paz's best analogy for this collective liberation arises when he links the Revolution with a fiesta. He perceptively evokes the actual, sad, Mexican village fiesta where the oppressed Mexican discharges his accumulated anguishes. But Paz, reading his anthropologists well (Roger Caillois, Lévy-Bruhl, and Mircea Eliade are cited in the book), sees behind this actual fiesta a blueprint of a fiesta that could be. Just as behind the actual, violent, sordid Mexican Revolution, lay another potential revolution. Sometimes these two fiestas or two revolutions coincide within an individual. Paz's potential fiesta is first of all the "advent of the unexpected" (L, 41); the exception that reverses or abolishes all the taboos and laws controlling everyday life. The fiesta inaugurates an "enchanted world" (L, 42); mythic time, pure actuality, untouched by history. Paz compares this release to that of a dream: "it lightens us of our burden of time and reason" (L, 42). All order is subverted, all is permitted. Social hierarchies, habits, sexual differences all evaporate. Paz labels the fiesta the reign of *caprichos* (whims); children and fools govern. In this fiesta man participates, in the Lévy-Bruhl sense. In Paz's ideal fiesta a *revuelta* (revolt/return), in its etymological sense, takes place and restores what Paz calls *vida pura* (pure life), a metaphor of an experience that transcends categories and flows into terms like original liberty, reunion, returns to a prenatal or presocial state, a beginning. A fiesta liberates man as does a surrealist happening. Paz's *ser* suggests a baptism in the "original disorder." Paz had experienced this fiesta in Spain. If one reduces all Paz says to a chain of analogies— unexpected, whim, exception, enchanted world, myth, pure life, pure actuality, revolt, participation, children, madmen, disorder etc.—we have a description of surrealist values.

Paz's version of love clarifies these values. His idea of love, a moral vision adopted from André Breton, promises salvation from the prison of history by positing man's other, woman, for human nature "consists in aspiring to realize oneself in the other" (L, 35). Love abolishes solitude, self-centeredness, the individual, and ushers in the experience of wholeness through the communion of two opposites (man and woman), a metaphor of the liberation of the individual into a collectivity. So Paz's Bretonian view of love differs from the Mexican norm by basing itself on the mutuality of desire. Few people abandon themselves to the other to go beyond the pleasurable, possessive stage (endemic to the Mexican macho) and grasp what love really is within the lover: "a perpetual discovery, an immersion in the waters of reality and a constant recreation" (L,

35). Love as an immersion in reality completes the analogy between love and the fiesta, for lovers contact their *ser*, origins and roots. In Mexico this difficult love becomes inaccessible; Mexicans negate this "bit of true life." In his 1959 appendix Paz writes: "Everything is opposed to it: morality, classes, laws, races and the very lovers themselves" (*L*, 163). Paz's love is a metaphor of free choice and thus freedom—and he cites Breton in support—impossible in the Mexico of the 1950s because of its inflexible sexist images, taboos, and laws. For the Mexicans, this surrealist love can only be a scandal, a transgression of their law. Paz joins the surrealist attacks on the ideas of original sin, marriage, and family. Paz ends his frenetic defense of love as a value in this appendix in a passage reminiscent of the surrealist manifestos: "To defend love has always been a dangerous antisocial activity. And now [he writes in 1959] it begins to be truly revolutionary. The situation of love in our time reveals how the dialectics of solitude . . . tends to frustrate itself thanks to society itself. Our social life nearly always denies authentic erotic communion" (*L*, 167).

Replace "love" with "poetry" and you would find an identical difficulty, due to a bourgeois society locked into alienating solitude, victim of history. Defending love began as a critique of its absence in Mexico and spread to include all contemporary societies. It is the theme of his 1948 poem "El prisionero" and many of the prose poems of *¿Aguila o sol?* (*Eagle or Sun?*, 1951). Defending life was Paz's motto for those days in Paris.

At the core of Paz's moral vision lies a belief (tested and confirmed in Spain and later among the surrealists) that history will one day end: "We all hope that society will return to its original freedom and men to their primitive purity. Then history will cease" (*L*, 175). The sources to this seemingly idealist stance might be Rousseau or Nietzsche, but are also experiential. Paz has interpreted a fundamental metaphor: during the act of love between a man and a woman social, historical, and cultural identities dissolve in the "explosion" of reality that is the orgasm. Paz subversively has pinned man's identity to that ecstatic experience whose intensity is a glimpse of paradise. So he brushes aside sociological, psychological, historical, biological, and cultural definitions. This experience cannot be proved or disproved; it is an inner experience of liberation. Paz's 1959 appendix bitterly criticizes European rationality that has imprisoned man in a mirror-lined torture chamber. The dreams of

European reason are atrocious (the atomic bomb). Paz's solution is to dream "with eyes closed" (L, 176), awake to the liberating inner world. He aggressively directs his wisdom at both the Mexican nationalists and at the Marxists and wants them to share his vision that men are "orphans of the past" and have to invent, that is, create, their future. And Paz insists on his contemporaneity with the Europeans: "Europe, that store of ready-made ideas, lives now like us: from day to day" (L, 176). The war had terminated Europe's glamor and prestige; Paz was one of the first to sense this ending of a long cultural hegemony. This liberation allowed him to befriend Breton as a Mexican, that is, as an equal. For Mexico was no longer exotic, inferior, or backward but equally alienated, anguished, and lost as France. El laberinto de la soledad, written in Paris, confirms this personal liberation in a veiled way as much as being written to wake up his fellow Mexicans to the modern situation. The artist's duty is to help others "recover their consciousness" (H, 12).

¿Aguila o sol?

Following the hectic writing of El laberinto de la soledad, Paz's ¿Aguila o sol?, one of his most innovative books, employs an aggressive Mexican title. These prose poems fuse the discovery and recovery of pre-Columbian and childhood Mexico with his experience as a surrealist in Paris, especially a liberating reading of Henri Michaux. Both ¿Aguila o sol? and El laberinto de la soledad overlap in the fundamental idea of a buried Mexico, and a search for roots and origins. The Antonio Machado epigraph to El laberinto de la soledad about man's essential heterogeneity or many conflicting selves, applies equally to the frantic self-dialogues that sustain many of these prose poems. Paz dramatizes the notion that history happens inside the poet's mind which becomes the "battle field" (P, 224) of his period.

The Mexican painter Rufino Tamayo (1899–) illustrated the first edition. Tamayo, a crucial figure of the Contemporáneos generation whose reaction to the militant political content of the muralists in favor of an art aspiring to a universal appeal, became an "example of moral and artistic intrepidity" (Pe, 251). In the 1930s Villaurrutia had defended Tamayo's attempt to combine his essential mexicanidad with the international language of painting. In 1950 Tamayo won the Venice Biennale and exhibited in Paris where André Breton

wrote a laudatory catalog presentation. Breton described his art as
one that caressed eyes and crackled with life; a painting of things
never seen before, celebrating the instant: in Tamayo's world man
had stayed in contact with the forces of nature.[38] From Paris Paz
also wrote his first piece on Tamayo (1950). As a fellow Mexican,
sharing Tamayo's intentions, he could only enthuse. Paz highlighted
the limitations of ideological art and argued that Tamayo's art was
an exorcism, "an instinctive answer to the pressure of history,"
revealing man's most secret (i.e., inner) vision (*Pe,* 263). He selected
the "solar element," Tamayo's tropical exuberance (opposed to the
grey Parisian context), as most characteristic, linking his title *¿Aguila
o sol?* with Tamayo. Paz's enthusiasm reveals his own artistic intentions. He has often written on Tamayo's art, editing a book in
1959, with long articles in 1960 and 1968. Tamayo stands for the
immediate vision; the world glimpsed for the first time; and art as
a process of inner search, a "seeking one's self" (*Pu,* 221).

"Ser natural" (Natural being), a prose poem in three parts in
homage to Tamayo, alludes to the telluric qualities in his art pointed
out by Breton. This prose poem later became a catalog presentation
(1967). It describes Tamayo's colorist world—blues, greens, pinks,
embodying an archetypal drama involving the moon, guitars, clocks
and watermelons, in a world where "we glimpse our portion of
totality" (*P,* 223). The second section describes another painting
about lovers where art liberates the inner life and "reality wakes up,
breaks out of its shell, extends its wings and flies" (*P,* 223). Paz's
poem doubles the paintings, criticism has become re-creation, the
dead language of interpretation redeemed, the world renewed. This
liberating function of gazing at art has led Paz to write many poems
about other artists, not as aesthetic appreciation but as moral examples offering "moments" of liberation from the pressures of history.

¿Aguila o sol? celebrates both Paz's own *ruptura* with his earlier
lyrical poems and his discovery through surrealism that art can be
an action, an alternative to a political one, that liberates the inner
man and fights for a world where art's effects are available to all,
thus abolishing art. The Mexican title refers to a coin with the eagle
that symbolized the founding of the Aztec Empire (a sophisticated
civilization owing nothing to Europe) and the sun (Tamayo's element) that was the heart of their cosmology. The question that the
title asks: eagle or sun—the spinning of a coin—suggests an ar-
bitrary choice, either way leading to the literal language of societal

discourse. The poet disposes of this duality (the binary structure of language, the gap between sign and signifier) by invoking a new inner art that fuses opposites into the experience of unity: "the eagle is sun" (*Arco*, 99). In a preface Paz contrasted his earlier, adolescent poetry with his new found responsibilities: "Hoy lucho a solas con una palabra" (today I fight alone with a word, *P*, 163). Conscious of the infection of history, he fights like a solitary for the word beyond "language" that grants freedom. The tone of that phrase conveys a man to man duel where a word might annihilate the poet. This terrifying *lucha* taps the 1950s mood in Paris where the poet's role was to be on guard, alert, the enemy already inside him, corrupting the very language he uses.

This collection breaks with Paz's past poetry by being in prose: prose poems that verge on essays, allegories, parables, manifestos, and short stories. Paz's break with the typographical conventions of lyrical poetry is his attempt to capture real poetry. Because the prose poem is a seemingly "open" form—it allows all kinds of things to intrude, more vulnerable to chance and the unconscious and closer to the spirit of automatic writing—it appears to be more modern. The tradition of the prose poem begins with Baudelaire, and passes to Rimbaud, Lautréamont, and Mallarmé, to catch the frantic movement and crowding of the industrialized city-experience: "the prose poem expresses the poetry of modern life" (*Pe*, 70). In his 1979 *Poemas* Paz included his prose play and a prose essay *El mono gramático* (The monkey grammarian). For poetry is not locked into aesthetic forms and rhythms, but is an experience, a relationship between the reader and a text. In 1966 Paz declared: "There is no prose" for "everything is poetry in language" (*Po*, 16).[39] It is all a question of the intensity of vision, the opening out of the plurality innate in language, a liberation.

Paz divided *¿Aguila o sol?* into three sections. The first "Trabajos del poeta" (Works of the poet, 1949) hints at the poet's working notes, his botched versions, a kindling similar to automatic writing where, as Breton affirmed, inspiration comes after. Paz indulges in a personal, anguished duel with language where the real poem happens off-page, inside the poet; the transformation or momentary liberation of the poet himself. The sixteen subsections personify language in a tone suggesting a pitiless battle with the poet's life at stake. Close to Henri Michaux, this ferocious activity and continuous metamorphoses of language-matter threatens and disturbs:

"Los hay de una sola cabeza y quince patas. Otros son nada más rostro y cuello. Terminan en un triángulo afilado. Cuando vuelan, silban como silba en el aire el cuchillo. Los jorobados son orquestas ambulantes e infinitas. . . . Las bellas arrastran con majestad largas colas de babas. . . . Son innumerables e innombrables" (There are some with only one head and fifteen paws. Others are nothing but face and neck. They end in a pointed triangle. When they fly they whistle like a knife in the air. The hunchbacks are itinerant and infinite orchestras. . . . The beauties drag majestic long trains of slime. . . . They are numerous and unnamable, P, 166). The controlling metaphor is the poet hunting for the word, seeking inspiration. By section 6—the *ars poetica* of this part—the fight for the word has led the poet to desert his friends, reasonable women, literature, morality, beautiful verse, pyschology, and novels in his quest for freedom. This becomes an ascetic purge of alienated language inside the poet: "se rompen los lazos con el mundo, la razón y el lenguaje" (the ties with the world, reason and language are broken, P, 169). Once emptied the poet can but wait: "Vaciado, limpiado de la nada purulenta del yo, vaciado de tu imagen, ya no eres sino espera y aguardar" (emptied, cleansed of the purulent nothingness of your ego, emptied of your image, you are nothing but hoping and waiting, P, 169). Then the Word appears, like a bird: "El pájaro es feroz y acaso te sacará los ojos" (the bird is ferocious and may poke out your eyes, P, 169). The last eight sections fill out this state of waiting and encounter with the bird with the poet daydreaming, sleeping, and writing, conscious of the need for this purge of corrupt language: "vómito de palabras, purgación del idioma infecto. . . . Devuelvo todas las palabras, todas las creencias, toda esa comida fría con que desde el principio nos atragantan" (vomit of words, purge of infected language. . . . I throw up all the words, beliefs, all that cold food which since the beginning they have choked us with, P, 173). The rotten times demand a new language (poetry) that abolishes the corruptors of language, and Paz lists them surrealistically: families, temples, libraries, prisons, brothels, factories, revolution, faith: the enemies of poetry.

Once the destructive purge is achieved, the poet may journey "inward" (P, 174); traveling through the dead mineral matter accumulated in his pysche. By subsection sixteen the poet has arrived at his freedom: a dense section packed with archetypal and natural analogies for the thrill of freedom: river of diamonds, blue cascade, bird, lightning, fountain of fire feathers, star. The last words describing this inner state are "infinite" and "anonymous" (*P*, 177), the bedrock of being where everybody is equal, universal.

"Trabajos del poeta" works excitingly by combining the poet's intentions with the actual chaotic process or journey toward consciousness of inner liberation in an age that has poisoned the language of poetry itself. Paz has begun his journey toward the Mallarmean notion that the twentieth-century poet is primarily a critic who demolishes, not only the prevalent institutions and moralities but language itself, before creating. Often this critical act is the poem. The poet thus becomes a guide by discriminating what is infected from what still lives. Paz's prison of history, the labyrinth of solitude, appears less tragic: there is a way out. In the last section "Hacia el poema" (Toward the poem), the poem that can never be written because it is the inner experience of lucid liberation, Paz writes: "We turn and turn in the animal stomach, the mineral stomach, the temporal stomach. To find the way out: the poem" (*P*, 228). But note the infinitive "to find," because rebirth must always be refought for, there is no permanent state of liberation, only the instant of the experience itself.

The second main section "Arenas movedizas" (Quicksand), dated 1949, combining echoes of T. S. Eliot's sterile desert with the trickiness of the inner life, opens with "El ramo azul" (The blue bouquet), a prose poem, almost a short story, as bafflingly rich as a dream.

As a narrative the story subverts its title's associations of blue bouquet with innocence and lovers. Realistically set in a tropical Mexican pueblo, where the narrator wakes up at night in his inn, feels like having a cigarette, and walks off into the deserted pueblo until he senses somebody following him. There follows a conversation in realistic Mexican dialect between an Indian peasant and the narrator whose eyes are wanted as a bouquet for the Indian's novia. The narrator pleads, but the Indian is relentless: "It's a whim of my fiancée's. She wants a little bunch of blue eyes" (*P*, 179). The narrator is made to kneel; he stares at the machete and has a light held up to his eyes. Then the Indian realizes his mistake: "Well they are not blue, sir. Please forgive me" (*P*, 180), that politeness a masterly touch. The narrator struggles back to his inn and flees the village.

At this level this story's macabre realism suggests a nightmare. However, Paz's Parisian context opens up other meanings. The surrealists adored unpredictable Mexico. So Paz served them up this other, invisible Mexico, alive to Goyaesque *caprichos*, a genuinely threateningly surreal country.[40] Paz returned to this tropical other Mexico, nostalgically, to convince the Parisian surrealists that he belonged to a real surreal place not overcivilized, grey Paris. But more than catering to an exotic view of Mexican peasantry, this story also plays with the notion "poet." Who are the real poets in Mexico? Here the story breaks into a parable about the hostile other, the stubborn, reticent peasant inside Paz. A parable dramatizing a clash between the cosmopolitan and the indigenous inside Paz himself. In 1984 Paz wrote: "The Indian world. It is a dimension of my country both intimate and unfathomable, familiar and unknown. Without it we would not be who we are" (*H*, 12). Exploring the narrator further we learn that he is a sophisticated city dweller, scared of scorpions and insects. As he walks away from his inn he has learned thoughts: "I thought that the universe was a vast system of signs, a conversation between immense beings. My acts, the cricket's sawing, the blinking of stars were but pauses and syllables, dispersed phrases of that dialogue" (*P*, 179). The world as a forest of symbols refers to Baudelaire's famous sonnet "Correspondances."[41] This narrator/learned poet could be an aspect of Paz himself. This poet is then faced with a peasant who acts out a *capricho*. Isn't acting out a whim a surrealist ideal? Isn't the peasant more of a natural poet, in the surrealist *acte gratuite* sense, than the narrator? This whole parable depends on blue eyes and blue eyes are foreigner's eyes. Fortunately, the learned poet-narrator did not possess blue eyes; he does belong to this nightmare world after all, though he does not dare explore any further into this pueblo and in an act of cowardice flees: "The next day I fled from that village" (*P*, 180). And Paz in reality does have blue eyes! The link between the Europeanized, elitist poet and the silent natural peasant poet is strong and dynamic, for this duel takes place inside Paz, discovering his roots in Paris. The story illustrates a fear of the hostile, mysterious, violent "other." What Paz has called "My fear of confronting reality" (*L*, 10). Paz's privilege over the Parisian surrealists was that he could still make contact with his primitive roots, or as Breton wrote about Tamayo, the "forces" of nature.

What characterizes the Mexican is that the past epochs, even the remotest, are still alive as wounds inside him. "El ramo azul" narrates this perception dramatically as a nightmare. It is in this sense that we read *El laberinto de la soledad* as a confession: the *pachuco*, the *macho*, the *indio* are alive in all Mexicans, Paz included. This is the appeal and mystery of *lo mexicano*, especially the peasant (Indian) of chapter 4 who is strange, imperturbable, and ancient, especially for Europeans.

The Indian relativizes the poet's recourse to European poetic universality by demanding a bouquet of blue eyes. The *indio* is the other. Identity and liberation are consequences of this dialogue between the self and the other. This dialogue surfaces in "Encuentro" (Encounter), a prose poem approaching the subtlety of Borges's "Borges y yo" (of *El hacedor*)[42] and alluding to Henri Michaux's subversive philosophical playfulness (especially in *Mes propriétés*).[43] "Encuentro" denies the encounter of its title. The supposed meeting becomes a deepening of confusions. The Michaux tone emerges from the first sentence: "When I arrived at my house, precisely at the moment of opening the door, I saw myself leave" (*P*, 202). The narrator follows himself and they begin to chat in a bar. But this "other" refuses to recognize the narrator and they squabble, shout, and insult each other. Humiliated and rejected, the narrator walks home. The text ends like Borges's: "On the way I had a doubt that still keeps me awake, what if he was not he, but me?" (*P*, 204).

The third main section of *¿Aguila o sol?*, called "¿Aguila o sol?" contains variants on this topic of the other. The other is the poet's childhood, or Mexico's pre-Columbian past, or a woman, or poetry itself.

Paz described this book to Rita Guibert as a "little book in which the pre-Columbian world appears as part of my own psychological subsoil."[44] Inside Paz coexist superimposed epochs like geological strata (a debt to Freud) and all of them alive. "Mariposa de obsidiana" (Obsidian butterfly) brilliantly illustrates this notion. First published in French in 1950,[45] it betrays a vital context that shows that this pre-Columbian cosmology appealing to European fantasy and an alternative to Christianity still survived in Mexicans like Paz. The poem is aggressively Mexican; in Paris Paz did not contrive to be cosmopolitan. When published in Mexico, this prose poem told Mexicans that surrealism had allowed Paz to recover a truly Mexican, erotic muse. The learned footnote to the poem displays Paz's originality, for he has to explain the obsidian butterfly to both

French and Mexican readers. He has interpreted a vague Aztec goddess Itzpapálotl, confused with Teteoinan and Tonatzin, to end: "all these female divinities have been united in the cult devoted to the Guadalupe virgin since the sixteenth century" (P, 214). In El laberinto de la soledad he had bared the fanatic cult of this virgin in relation to Tonatzin. About this same obsidian butterfly Irene Nicholson stated hesitantly: "she seems to represent those delights that man, fallen from grace, has been deprived of."[46] Paz removes that "seems" and makes those forgotten delights the center of his prose poem.

From Paris Paz recovered a Mexico that he had gleaned from books. The recent discovery of the Aztec past, especially Nahuatl poetry, could not assume a lived relationship between present-day Mexico and its past. The Mexican's break with the colonial period had forced him to work hard to define his tradition. Paz's footnote details his worry that readers might miss his erudite analogies and intentions. For the obsidian butterfly is "our mother" (P, 214). Paz proposed to reawaken Mexico to its "mother." In El laberinto de la soledad he had explored this mother, using the device of asking her a question: "If we question the third figure of the triad, the Mother, we will hear a double answer. . . . First, it is to do with an Indian virgin; then, the place of her apparition . . . is a hill that before had been a sanctuary dedicated to Tonatzin, our mother, the Aztec goddess of fertility" (L, 71). Paz elaborates on the defeat of this fertility goddess during the Conquest. His 1951 prose poem flows from this question, but here the poet listens to what she has to say. The diosa (goddess) narrates the poem, speaking to the poet from within him, like a muse dictating her lament and remedy. The poet is privileged to hear her message; it is part of his awakening into the peculiar consciousness of being a Mexican. The poem opens: "Mataron a mis hermanos, a mis hijos, a mis tíos. A la orilla del lago de Texcoco me eché a llorar. Del Peñón subían remolinos de salitre. Me cogieron suavemente y me depositaron en el atrio de la Catedral. Me hice tan pequeña y tan gris que muchos me confundieron con un montón de polvo" (They killed my brothers, my sons, my uncles. On the shore of Lake Texcoco I burst into tears. From the Peñón rose clouds of saltpeter. They grabbed me softly and deposited me in the porch of the cathedral. I made myself so small, so grey that they confused me with a heap of dust, P, 214–15). The "they," the Conquistadores with their European catholic faith, are seen as an antilife force where the goddess's fate-heap of dust-mirrors the drying up of the lake around Tenochtitlán. But Paz has noticed her and she can remind him of who she was before the Conquest: "Si, yo misma, la madre del pedernal y de la estrella, yo, encinta del rayo, soy ahora la pluma azul que abandona el pájaro en la zarza. Bailaba, los pechos en alto y girando, girando, girando hasta quedarme quieta; entonces empezaba a echar hojas, flores, frutos" (yes I myself, mother of flint and star, I, pregnant by lightning, am now the blue feather abandoned by the bird in the bramble. I danced, breasts in the air, turning, turning, turning until I was still; then I began to sprout leaves, flowers, fruit, *P*, 215). She appropriates the creative fires (flint, lightning, star) in her erotic fertility dance. She speaks to the poet in a language dense with metaphors in sentences packed with analogies as if the "poetry" she speaks is the original language. A long paragraph re-creates this imagistic richness, ending with her lament about the years of neglect. A litany of two sentences beginning with "I am tired . . . ," then four with "Lucky . . . ," then two with "When . . . ," builds up a rhythm of isolation and despair. She then instructs the poet how to resuscitate her by touching her breasts and kissing her belly to announce oracularly: "De mi cuerpo brotan imágenes: bebe en esas aguas y recuerda lo que olvidaste al nacer" (from my body images sprout: drink in those waters and remember what you forgot when you were born, *P*, 216). Paz, a Mexican, is closer to the origins, can still drink at this source and remember—the Platonic notion and the same stress on consciousness. This baptism confirmed Paz as both Mexican and poet. The prose poem ends: "Allí abrirás mi cuerpo en dos, para leer las letras de tu destino" (there you will open my body in two to read the letters of your destiny, *P*, 216). Paz was destined to be the poet who remembered his origins, his mother, his identity.

From Paris, resolving his crisis about the kind of action that poetry demanded, Paz also returned to his personal past in Mexico, as a magical land (in contrast with war-torn Europe). "La higuera" (The fig tree), derives from a crucial personal symbol invoked in many later poems. The prose poem states its location, Mixcoac, where Paz was brought up and a fig-tree with which he obscurely identified (Mother Nature, natural, sensual wisdom). This fig-tree knocked on his window calling him out to life. He would climb its jade branches like a green ship, his head standing out "crowned

with prophecies" for this female, D. H. Lawrence tree had initiated
him into poetry. The jade tree then reads out his destiny in a litany
of dense sentences beginning with "Te prometo . . ." (I promise
you), promising him a vision. The poem ends with a sarcastic
dilemma: "Hoy la higuera golpea en mi puerta y me convida. ¿Debo
coger el hacha o salir a bailar con esa loca?" (today the fig-tree
knocks at my door and invites me. Should I get my axe or go out
and dance with that mad woman?, P, 218). As a poet, he must
dance with his muse, the *loca*. Surrealism, a madness in the eyes of
society, had made this dancing a moral imperative; the poet had to
fight to affirm his vision.

Paz's years in Paris witness an immense gain in lucidity as a poet
in a hostile world. The delightful prose poem "Dama Huasteca"
(Huastec lady) amplifies this self-confidence, its title hints at a
Mexican muse, the *dama* harking back to the troubador's courtly
love, the *huasteca* to an East Coast branch of the Maya from whom
the Aztecs adopted a goddess of carnal love. Irene Nicholson describes her as Chalchihuitlicue, elder sister of the rain goddess,
painted blue and yellow with turquoise ear plugs and quetzal feathers. Her skirt and shift are painted like water.[47] Paz enlarges this
"water" (erotic, fertility) quality. In his poem she is "naked," just
"bathed," covered in "jewels." She is associated with sexuality,
volcanoes, eagles, and water. Archetypal woman, but "few have seen
her" (P, 222), except the poet. His duty is to speak for her: "Diré
su secreto" (I will tell her secret, P, 222), an echo of Rimbaud's
"Je dirai son secret" and a tradition of *poètes mages* that Paz joins.[48]
The poem ends with a revelation: "de día es una piedra al lado del
camino; de noche, un río que fluye al costado del hombre" (by day
she is a stone by the side of the road; by night a river that flows
by man's side, P, 222). It is the poet who recognizes this anonymous
inert "stone" (a recurrent symbol of opacity and numbness of society,
language, etc.)[49] and at night, through his imagination, he transforms her into an erotic companion, a river in his waste land,
inspiration. The poet redeems this goddess and locates his own poetic
fertility.

In the late 1940s Paz found his identity, consolidated his activity
to change inner man and thus future action. "Himno futuro" (Future
hymn) postulates a "free man" and refreshing, fertilizing water:
"¡ Agua, agua al fin, palabra del hombre para el hombre!" (water,
water at last, word of a man for man!, P, 227). It is this purified

moral word or poetry that ushers in the new society of men com-
muning with each other without gods, bosses, or ideologies. The
last section of ¿Aguila o sol?, called "Hacia el poema" (Toward the
poem) and subtitled "points of departure," enriches this notion of
future activity. It fuses aphorisms, instructions, and manifestos in
a Nietszchean way. The topics covered include woman, dreaming,
the abstract twentieth-century realities, fantasy, language, love, the
other, all in terms of the "new dialogue," the new "amorous order"
that poetry rather than politics was preparing in the 1940s. His
penultimate aphorism reiterates the last paragraph of El laberinto de
la soledad and the last line of "Himno entre ruinas" offering the
same hopeful activity ushered in by surrealism: "When history sleeps,
it speaks in dreams: in the forehead of the sleeping people the poem
is a constellation of blood. When history wakes up, the image
becomes an act, the poem happens: poetry enters into action" (P,
230). This is Paz's newfound wisdom. The awakening of the poet
to history's invasion of his soul allows him to react. The "into action"
has a military ring to it for poems are revolutionary and change
consciousness.[50] Paz applies Marxist terms to the inner aesthetic
experience, just as in 1935 Breton had sought to fuse Rimbaud and
Marx in his revolution.[51]

   "Un poeta" (A poet) explicitly deals with "poetry" being urban
man's salvation from alienation and the abuses of power. The poem
consists of two parts, the second in italics, and offers two opposing
views of the poet's urgent social and ethical duties. The first part
deals with the "surrealist" poet exploring his inner space. It states
its ideal where the poet becomes his poem in a society of poets,
abolishing written poems and all social divisions. The insinuation:
writing poems in the 1940s seemed a practical step toward a future
where the solitary, marginalized act of writing (and reading) would
be abolished: "Knowing is not different from dreaming and dreaming from doing" (P, 221). No more barriers; a total consciousness
that fuses all these activities into a new life-style and society. In
the 1940s Marxism had forced poets like Paz to situate poetry in a
social context. Paz ends this section: "Poetry has set fire to all the
poems. Finished with words, finished with images. The distance
between the name and the thing abolished, to name is to create and
to imagine to be born" (P, 221). Poetry has returned to its natural
paradisaical origins: language (and the poet) no longer alienated.
   The second italicized section brings in the dilemma facing Paz,

but the tone is ironic as Paz has rejected this option as sterile. It
opens with a party order: *"Meanwhile, grab a spade, theorize, be punc-
tual" (P,* 221). Here the poet's revolutionary worth is berated, he
must be more useful, do manual work, read Marx, discuss politics,
be up to date, and read the newspapers so that his tongue becomes
swollen with politics (*P,* 221).[52] The only consequence of this option
is dishonor (Péret's 1945 attack on politicized poets *Le déshonneur
des poètes*)[53] or condemnation (Stalin's gulags). What the poet needs
in this view of his social usefulness is a *"strong philosophy"* (i.e.,
Marxism). But by this date Paz had opted for the first version of
"Un poeta."

La estación violenta

Paz collected poems written in the 1940s and 1950s in *La estación
violenta* (1958; The violent season, written 1948–53), arranging the
poems in chronological order. The earliest is "Himno entre ruinas",
dated 1948. In the same year Paz traveled to Italy, visiting Venice,
Naples, and Sicily. "Máscaras del alba" (Dawn masks) is situated
in the San Marcos piazza, with specific references to the place, yet
becoming a poem about the collapse of empires, the end of European
hegemony and capitalism, and doubt about redemption from this
reality: "Bosteza lo real sus naderías, / se repite en horrores desven-
trados" (reality yawns its nothingnesses, / repeats itself in disem-
boweled horrors, *P,* 236). This is the 1940s world of "dead alive."
Paz's title, *La estación violenta,* deliberately alluded to that historical
epoch, the cold-war violence, in this poem epitomized in Venice
with its festival masks. Paz confessed to Carballo that Venice was
so fantasmal that at dawn it broke up.[54] The last line conveys this
ephemeral quality: "El alba lanza su primer cuchillo" (*P,* 238); the
light of nature wipes out the "unreal" city (Paz adopts T. S. Eliot's
view in *The Waste Land* of the city as symbol of history, twentieth-
century corruption).[55]

"Repaso nocturno" (Nocturnal review), dated Paris, 1950, has
an insomniac (a recurrent persona with Paz) reviewing his grim
period; the absence of solutions to his dilemmas as a dialogue with
his own consciousness with Paris as a possible site for poetry's entering into action, but the poem ends in despair, an empty mirror,
the cold eye "no hay nada que decir" (there is nothing to say, *P,*
243). For a moment poetry does not lead to any change.

"Fuente" (Fountain), written in Avignon, 1950, draws its power from the special role of the poet as harbinger of the new life. When the poem first appeared its title "Segunda vigilia" continued Paz's occasional series "Vigilias" (Vigils), a metaphor of the poet awake, alert, not falling asleep.[56] This vigil suggests the poet as a hero, but at a great personal sacrifice because he does not belong to those in power. Paz's poet-hero could redeem modern decadence in his song: but he has been expelled from the city.[57] The city-state, the Platonic expulsion of the poets. Paz was answering Plato back. In this poem the city of Avignon is precisely evoked with its walls, towers, palaces, market, and river in the pristine Provençal light to describe a moment of union between the poet and the city that turns into a false ephiphany. When the poet questions his vision, he receives no answer:

¿y el delirio de hacer saltar la muerte con el apenas golpe de alas de una
    imagen
y la larga noche pasada en esculpir el instantáneo cuerpo del relámpago
y la noche de amor puente colgante entre esta vida y la otra?

                                                                    (P, 240)

(and the delirium of blowing up death with the hardly a wing blow of an image / and the long night spent in sculpting the instantaneous body of lightning / and the night of love bridge hanging between this life and the other?)

The poet's fight for poetry and love as antidotes to spiritual death seemed in crisis. Then he catches sight of a fountain and realizes that the poet sacrifices himself so that others (his readers) may learn and act. The poem ends: "En el centro de la plaza la rota cabeza del poeta es una fuente. / La fuente canta para todos" (in the center of the square the poet's broken head is a fountain. / The fountain sings for everybody, P, 241). If history "breaks" the poet as transient individual, his song survives and helps to found the new society where everybody turns poet, restoring his social position to the center of the square and inspiration to the center of life. This sacrifice forms part of Paz's anti-ego, antipersona stance.[58] In 1951 he wrote "All poems fulfill themselves at the poet's expense" (P, 229). For man's life escapes a historical definition: "my real history is other" (P, 240).

In 1950, in Paris, introducing a collection of Mexican poetry in translation, Paz defined his view of poetry in the 1950s: "The poem continues to be an exorcism capable of preserving us from the spell of power, number, and ambiguity. Poetry is one of the forms available to modern man to say no to all the powers that not only decide our lives, but also our consciousness" (*Pe*, 37).

In 1952 Paz visited India and Japan, a preliminary foray into an alternative culture providing him with further comparisons between the United States, Mexico, and Paris. Though Paz traveled in person, he had already traveled as a reader. For example in New York (1945) he had rediscovered José Juan Tablada's Far Eastern poetry (*El jarro de flores*, 1922; *Li-Po*, 1920) and was responsible for situating Tablada as the founder, with Ramón López Velarde, of Mexican poetry in movement, his expression for how in an anthology he viewed the Mexican poetic tradition in terms of the present relevance and not as an accepted succession of best poems.[59] Tablada had initiated Paz into the adventure of reading, "into knowing how to abandon my native city" (*Pe*, 88).

Paz abandoned Mexico in many senses over those years of exile. But as a literary traveler he also returned to Mexico, in print, with essays (in 1954, "Three Moments of Japanese Literature") and translations (mainly from the English of Waley, Keene, and Blyth). He read deeply in Zen, Buddhism, Tantra, Chinese painting, and the No theater and became fascinated with Bashō, translating his haikus and *Sendas de Oku* in 1957.

Literary and personal travel further sharpened Paz's awareness of the poet as a universal value, equally despised and marginalized in Japanese culture as in his own. Surrealism's defiance against the *naderías* (nothingnesses) of the period seemed to Paz a universal position, not a parochial Parisian one. For example, Paz discovered that Bashō's playful version of writing paralleled the surrealist games (like the "exquisite corpse"); Bashō came close to Lautréamont's prediction about collective poetry, a haiku could "blow up apparent reality" (*Pe*, 160). Bashō's poetry is a "lived poetry," an invitation to change. Bashō's poetry throws man into the "marvelous" (Breton's favorite term), inside himself. Japanese literature, for all its particular cultural differences, confirmed Paz's belief that art "is an invitation to truly live life and poetry" (*Pe*, 164).

Two long poems develop Paz's first encounter with Asia: "Mutra"

(Delhi, 1952) and "¿No hay salida?" (Isn't there a way out?, Tokyo, 1952). "Mutra" is a crucial self-defining poem. The title places the poem in a town just south of Delhi and deals decisively with a "temptation to cede to Hindu or Buddhist mysticism."[60] Paz does not seek the "dissolution" of his consciousness, but its active involvement with historical life. The poem argues this decision in long sinuous lines. It opens with vivid imagistic approximations to India's heat ("mouths filled with hot insects," *P*, 244), beggars, bougainvillea, beautiful girls, fanatics, musicians, children, buzzards, monkeys; a shocked tourist's reactions given rich metaphorical equivalents. India betrays a "terrible cargamento de seres y de cosas" (a terrible loading of beings and things, *P*, 245). Faced with this vast overcrowded chaos Paz fears that all humanity is in the tunnel (that he had diagnosed in Paris), all lost and alienated in the "corridors" (cf. T. S. Eliot's "Gerontion"—history's contrived corridors)[61] of history (*P*, 245). From this sordid, fallen landscape Paz shifts into his innerscape ("Inside myself") to find in himself a ceaseless *estar* (being, but opposed to *ser*), a floating, movable life, adrift. Then Paz rejects this pure, vague inner world with a no! He defines himself against India: he wants to anchor his being in the poet dialoguing with history, not turning his back on life. Paz's model is the poet, not the saint. He prefers "el que da vida a las piedras de los muertos, el que hace hablar piedras y muertos" (he who gives life to the stones of the dead, he who makes the stones and dead talk, *P*, 246).

India's static beatitudes irritate him. He affirms "I am a man and a man is . . ." and he lists his view of man as an unfinished process, an exile, rootless, a bridge, an arch, split in two, an arrow "that never reaches itself": that is, in time, a creature in history. From affirming this temporal perspective Paz looks back on his own magical adolescence, as well as invoking the invigorating Mediterranean world (islands, women, goddesses, reflexive thought, geometry), the Western tradition: "el universo como una lira y un arco" (the universe like a lyre and a bow, *P*, 248), referring to Heraclitus's vital tension and his own later defense of poetry *El arco y la lira* (1956). Paz chooses the world of conflicts.

The poet returns from his thoughts to the moribund Indian city of Mutra flashing in the plain and opts for a Western solution: an action within the individual against history. An existential truth "man is only man among men" (*P*, 248), with its latent communal sense. In Delhi he plants the seed of growth and change, transience and historical time that will grow and change the poet.

"¿No hay salida?" regresses to Paz's recurrent questioning of the validity of poetry in the grim world of history with, in this poem, a momentary triumph of the antilife forces; there is no way out (of the tunnel, the labyrinth). In Tokyo, the insomniac poet's "thoughts" spin round and round in vicious circles. He cannot find the words—inspiration—to defend his insomnia (insomnia: history emptying the poet of inner resources like dreaming). In his hotel room life has shrunk to the shapes of cupboards, chairs, and ventilators. The poet is taunted by *allá* (over there), that somewhere else there is salvation (nights, river, lovers, bodies, poets) but denied to him in Japan: "Todo está lejos, no hay regreso, los muertos no están muertos, los vivos no están vivos, / hay un muro, un ojo que es un pozo, todo tira hacia abajo, pesa el cuerpo" (every thing is far away, there is no return, the dead are dead, the living do not live / there is a wall, an eye that is a well, all pulls down, the body weighs, *P*, 250–51). The poet, exiled in Tokyo, stuck in the present, cries out in anguish "qué sonido remoto tiene la palabra vida" (what a remote sound the word life has, *P*, 251). The alienated poet doubts his own existence: "Yo está aquí," divided from his self (cf. Rimbaud's "Je est un autre").[62]

In 1953, in Geneva, Paz met Ortega y Gasset and wrote "El río" (The river). This poem incorporates the Buddhistic notion of the destruction of the ego as necessary for the transmutation of the historically grounded individual into a poem, and its failure.[63] The outer city noise and bustle of Geneva enter the poet's head (as history invades each individual). Once inside his head the city tries to make sense of itself (the poet becomes a vehicle for this); "sus pedazos se buscan en mi frente, toda la noche la ciudad habla dormida por mi boca" (*P*, 252). At that moment the poet envies the Buddha's or the yogi's capacity to still this inner river (of thought), time flowing past too quickly. The poem explores the act of its own writing, but as a form of sterility, not liberation. He longs for the blessing of sleep and dreaming; the promise of writing a real poem. But he has nothing to say except "este escribir sobre lo escrito" (this writing about what is written, *P*, 253). His anguish is wanting to say something but instead repeating what the city of mindless noise says. Paz's fear is the loss of his visionary stance: "Nada ilumina el

opaco combate" (nothing illuminates the opaque combat, *P,* 254).
The poem ends in a moment of defeat, the poet tantalizingly aware
of his failed ambitions.

ABOUT THE AUTHOR

Jason Wilson is a visiting lecturer at King's College, University of London. His published works include scholarly articles on Vallejo, Borges, and Cortázar; reviews in the *Times Literary Supplement* (London), the *Modern Language Review*, the *Bulletin of Hispanic Studies*, and the *Journal of Latin American Studies*; and the critically acclaimed *Octavio Paz: A Study of His Poetics*. He resides in London with his wife.

Chapter Three

Return to Mexico

"El cántaro roto"

In 1953 Paz returned to Mexico after eleven years abroad, loaded with accumulated perceptions from his travels and readings and secure in his identity as a poet. Crucially, Paz went home in triumph, as a surrealist. Propagating his vision of the poet's revolutionary stance inevitably created a furor in the Mexico of the 1950s, still aggressively nationalistic. Paz's public activities during the 1950s must be seen within that prodigal-son context.

The shock of returning home as a surrealist poet (foreign poet) is conveyed powerfully and angrily in "El cántaro roto" (The broken jug, 1955) the last poem of *La estación violenta*. This long poem can be broken into several movements, each one plotting a journey to a moment of awareness culminating in Paz's belief in the revolutionary qualities of the inner space. The title reverts to archeology for its associations: the jug broken by history, the fragments that cannot be collected. The jug also holds the life-giving water; a *cántaro* is also a *canto*. In a more impassioned mode, the poem covers the same ground as "Himno entre ruinas." It is a litany against social oppression in Mexico and a manifesto about a remedy. The destructive forces of history never let up; the images are broken as T. S. Eliot wrote.[1]

The opening movement of the poem establishes the inner richness of the poet's mind: "La mirada interior se despliega y un mundo de vértigo y llama nace bajo la frente del que sueña" (the interior look opens out and a world of giddiness and flames is born under the forehead of he who dreams, *P, 255*). The dreamer's enchanted inscape: packed with vivid colors, flowers, sounds, birds, comets—flowing slowly like the long lines of the poem ending on an ecstatic exclamation mark. But Paz is ethically opposed to quietly cultivating his own inner garden. Poetic self-centeredness is insufficient. The poet's duty is social, to act out his inner vision.

The next movement has the poet opening his eyes to exterior

reality, the night stars, to contemplate this harmonious, thrilling world (but without man or time). This kind of easy ecstasy is also denied. In the third movement the poet descends to the Mexico of 1955: a desert of cactus, stones, heat. Paz condemns this literal and symbolic waste land in vivid images:

> No cantaba el grillo,
> había un vago olor a cal y semillas quemadas,
> las calles del poblado eran arroyos secos
> y el aire se habría roto en mil pedazos si alguien hubiese
>   gritado: ¿quien vive?
> Cerros pelados, volcán frío, piedra y jadeo bajo tanto
>   esplendor, sequía, sabor de polvo,
> rumor de pies descalzos sobre el polvo, ¡ y el pirú en medio
>   del llano como un surtidor petrificado!
>
> (*P*, 255–56)

(The cricket was not singing / there was a vague smell of lime and burned seed, / the village streets were dried streams / and the air would have broken into a thousand pieces if somebody would have screamed who lives? / bare hills, cold volcano, stone and panting under so much splendor, drought, taste of dust, / rumor of naked feet on dust and the piru cactus in the middle of the plain like a petrified fountain!)

This is precise, realistic description involving all the senses, with a vivid visual cactus—petrified fountain—but it is also a symbolic landscape invoking T. S. Eliot. In *The Waste Land* there are *dead trees giving no shade*, the *cricket no relief;* there are *dry stones, dust,* a baking *sun, stony rubbish, rocks* and *no water.*[2] You sense that Paz wanted to locate Eliot's waste land in Mexico, for in "The Hollow Men" Eliot had resorted to Mexican imagery—the dead land, the cactus land—to convey the spiritual emptiness of Western Man. By doing so Paz showed again that Mexico suffered the Western disease.

The poet questions this land of bones (again an Eliot allusion) wondering if there is any possibility of redemption, some water to restore life (Eliot had written; but there is no water). Paz's shocked despair, conveyed by the litanistic use of "only," is that he finds blood, dust, rags, insects, and heat. The poet asks marvelous questions: "¿No hay relinchos de caballos en la orilla del río, entre las grandes piedras redondas y relucientes . . . ?" (no whinnying of

horses by the river bank, between the great round shiny
stones . . . ?, *P*, 256). Paz's self-answer, the source of his invec-
tive, is that history has paralyzed Mexico: the past still lives, for if
the maize gods and virgins have vanished ("broken images"—T. S.
Eliot/"El cántaro roto"), the "toad" of power still remains: "¿sólo
el cacique gordo de Cempoala es inmortal?" (only the fat boss of
Cempoala is immortal?, *P*, 256). Cortés's ally against Moctezuma
leads to the betraying two-faced politicians who metamorphose
through the ages as the constant behind Mexican history, ending
up in the twentieth century, "los fines de semana en su casa blindada
junto al mar, al lado de su querida cubierta de joyas de gas neón"
(week ends in his bullet proof house next to the sea, next to his
mistress covered in neon gas jewels, *P*, 256). These tyrants have
created and maintain soulless Mexico (Paz is far more political than
Eliot and strives far harder to extricate man from this mess; no
nostalgia, no harking for some aristocratic order).

The next movement of the poem conveys this nightmare with
man degraded, turned into an insect, again in the form of a litany
("He aquí . . ."—Here is). But Paz has learned from the surrealists
how to exorcize this twentieth-century sterility.

The last twenty-two double lines (too long for the page) become
the poet's wisdom, his message. These lines must be read without
pause like a chant (there are no full stops) so that the dense saying
covers all the facets of his *sabiduría* that refuses to be compressed
into one image as it is a series of interlocked analogies. The meaning
is in the movement of analogy, not in the fixed thing itself. And
flow itself is a metaphor of liberation. The original language employed metaphors. What had been one line in "Himno entre ruinas"—*actos*—becomes here a frenzied manifesto, but the essence is
identical; act out the poet's vision as the ethical foundation of an
alternative society. This section begins:

Hay que dormir con los ojos abiertos, hay que soñar con las manos,
soñemos sueños activos de río buscando su cauce, sueños de sol soñando
sus mundos,
hay que soñar en voz alta, hay que cantar hasta que el canto eche raíces,
tronco, ramas, pájaros, astros,
cantar hasta que el sueño engendre y brote del costado del dormido la
espiga roja de la resurrección. . . .

                                                        (*P*, 258)

(We must dream with open eyes, we must dream with hands, / we must dream active dreams of rivers seeking their source, dreams of a sun dreaming its worlds / we must dream aloud, we must sing until the song grows roots, a trunk, branches, birds, stars, / we must sing until the dream engenders and sprouts from the dreamer's side with the red ear of grain of resurrection.)

This ending repeats the ending of *El laberinto de la soledad* (open eyes-dream, awareness).[3] It is the value of *cantar* (of poetry) that counts; a resurrection of despised values like love, woman, the dream, respect for the other. The whole stanza is supported by Paz's moral imperative *hay que*. And behind this lies Paz's socialist dream that only poetry could then achieve; a society of equals, without bosses, abuses of power, and repeating the viscious circle of history: "echar abajo las paredes entre el hombre y el hombre, juntar de nuevo lo que fue separado" (to knock down the walls between man and man, join again what had been separated, *P, 258*). What is fascinating in Paz's cascading ending is the movement that breaks up the succession of fixed "ideas" into sounds and echoes of ideas, making these ideas more sensual. The speed of movement parallels the vertigo of ecstasy. Thus Paz's ending is utopian, an ethical pretext for a poet's social utility, a critical stance against the Mexico of the 1950s, a plea for a revolutionary change from within, all at once.

The same, passionate, impatient, instructive tone can be detected in Paz's 1954 lecture on surrealism. He deliberately voiced a polemical, far from academic, version of surrealism, as a critique of the failings of Mexican artists to be truly revolutionary. Paz employs the "we" of the Parisian group and sets out his exposition in the postwar contexts of rigid ideologies and degradation of life. Only surrealism looked for the way out of the "collective slaughterhouse" (*Pe, 165*) of contemporary history, toward the true life. Surrealism defends imagination and desire, innate in man despite this society of robots. But above all, in 1954, Paz insisted that surrealism was not a dead corpse but, citing Breton's *Arcane 17* (1947), "the concrete exercise of freedom" (*Pe, 168*), a "putting into action of man's free disposition in a hand to hand fight with reality" (*Pe, 168*). Reality, the alienated world, a vast machine, Mexico. Surrealism was the only critical stance that also offered a way out.

Paz argued that all the surrealist techniques were attempts to

abolish this civilization's alienating grip on man to allow him to
recover his being and freedom. Only in this break from reality "are
we truly" (Pe, 170). This "being" denies all societal and historical
identity. Paz linked this with Buddhism, for the ecstatic break
opens the poet to all men tapping man's universal identity, whatever
his culture or moment in history. In 1954 Paz was clear that Breton's
rejection of a political revolution in favor of love as an attempt to
refind man's lost dignity and innocence would still work in spite
of the failure to usher in the new society. He affirms proudly "But
I know something" that surrealism would always be an invitation
to an inner adventure (Pe, 183). Paz had shifted surrealism from a
belief in group activity to that of the individual, like himself in
Mexico.

Elías Nandino's magazine Estaciones (1956–60) reacted hostilely
to Paz's lecture and stance. Nandino (1956) insisted that surrealism
was a dead end, passé, worthless as a model to follow and that
anybody (i.e., Paz) who tried to exercise it was a retrograde. He
politically condemned Paz as a reactionary Mexican.[4] Salvador Echevarría (1956) described surrealism as the apotheosis of stupidity,
a cheap conjuring trick, a poisonous and tragic thing. To be a
surrealist in Mexico of 1956 was to take an aimless course.[5] Salvador
Reyes Nevares (1956) actually named Paz as his target: surrealism
was antithetical to Mexican culture whose historic moment demanded a new realism.[6] Surrealism, in this Mexican context, had
changed meaning. In the 1950s it was frankly pejorative, and ap-
plied to Paz it insinuated that he was not a true revolutionary
Mexican but had been contaminated by European literature.[7]

Semillas para un himno

Paz's first collection of poems on returning to Mexico, the enigmatic and beautiful Semillas para un himno (Seeds for a hymn, 1954),
provoked further hostility. These poems seemed to be without subject matter, impervious to a circumstantial or committed position
and quite alien to what was happening in Mexico in the 1950s. If
we ignore Paz's silent dialogue with history within the poem, these
charges seem to fit. However, within the "cold hell" of those days,
these poems—seeds for the collective hymn of the new society—
aimed at describing and liberating those inner experiences that
resisted the contamination of history. These are dawn poems of hope

that these word-seeds will grow. Paz sought a new language, the obverse of history's discourse. The book rewrites Genesis and Darwinian evolution.

As an eighteen-year-old aspiring poet José Emilio Pacheco found these poems twisted and obscure in contrast to Paz's earlier, committed poetry. He blamed surrealism for contaminating Paz. Later, changing his mind radically, he referred to Paz as one of the great poets who had passed through surrealism. The period of the mid 1950s in Mexico had seen the term "surrealist" become the "forbidden word."[8] Many critics saw *Semillas para un himno* in similar terms: for Raúl Leiva the poems were hermetic, with a total loss of feeling and humanity.[9] Silva Villalobos found them inhuman and not Mexican.[10] The morally loaded word *contamination*, a defense of Mexican purity, on many critics's lips.[11] That surrealism could still provoke reactions in 1954 may surprise. Augusto Lunel, reviewing the same book, claimed that the term surrealist became an adjective for whatever could not be understood.[12] Yet for Paz himself it was a term of the highest praise. But Paz was not in isolation and received many generous critical notices (Ramón Xirau, Alí Chumacero).[13] Sides were being taken and Paz was becoming a leader of a group within Mexico.

The collection opens with a luminous glance at paradise. The intensely real natural world before man—evoked in "Himno entre ruinas"—fuses dawn, sunlight, and the sea. The poet is all eyes, looking at a world not yet deformed by human language, a world of marvelous potentials. In this paradisaical world (close to Vicente Aleixandre's *Sombra del paraíso* [Shadow of paradise, 1944])[14] of the origins there was no alienation. Between the desire and the act, an effortless step. The world was bound by interlocking metaphors, a fluid new world. The original metaphorical quality of language itself released from its twentieth-century straightjacket. In "Fábula" (Fable) we have: "La lluvia era un sauce de pelo suelto" (rain was a willow of loose hair, *P*, 134). No similes but direct reversible analogies: rain = willow = woman's hair. A perfect harmonious world. The poem continues:

> Había milagros sencillos llamados pájaros
> Todo era de todos
> Todos eran todo
> Sólo había una palabra inmensa y sin revés
> (*P*, 134)

(There was simple miracles called birds / Everything was everybody's / Everybody was everything / Only an immense word without another side.)

Everybody belonged to the world and the poem mirrors the fabulous sacred origins where all flows (no punctuation).

But this paradise shattered, and language created man's solitary, divided state by positing a fragmented world of unrelated, static, and dead things. The rest of the poem re-creates this fable, with its alluring possibilities of returning erotically to this origin through love repeating Adam and Eve in Eden: "El árbol la nube el relámpago / Yo mismo y la muchacha" (the tree cloud lightning / Myself and the girl, *P*, 135). For love taps this anonymous, innocent state again.

In "Cerro de la estrella" (Hill of the star) the word "naked" (of language, history) and the succession of verbs promising a return to the simple life conditions the process of liberation (again as in "Himno entre ruinas"): "Ver oír tocar oler gustar pensar" (to see hear touch smell taste think, *P*, 136). Cleansed by the senses, awaken by pleasure, man relearns how to think: thinking simply the awareness of being alive in the now of the world. This possibility of purification exists in the poet's capacity to reawaken "poetry" (uncontaminated language) inside himself. In "Manantial" (Source) we read:

> Agua clara vocales para beber
> Vocales para adornar una frente unos tobillos
> Habla
>   Toca la cima de una pausa dichosa
>   (*P*, 136–37)

(clear water vowels to drink / Vowels to adorn a forehead some ankles / Speak / Touch the peak of a joyful pause.)

Through reawakened sensations, and thus reawakened language (the poet transformed within himself in this inner adventure), the poet discovers true life:

> Pelo mano blancura no son nombres
> Para este pelo esta mano esta blancura
> Lo visible y palpable que está afuera

Lo que está adentro y sin nombre
A tientas se busca en nosotros
(*P*, 138)

(Hair hand whiteness are not names / For this hair this hand this whiteness / The visible and palpable that are outside / What is inside and without
name / Seek each other obscurely in Us.)

The dead language of history reanimated by purified sensations (*this*
hair),[15] is located in the "pause" that suspends time. The alien outer
world is transformed and given sense by the poet's inner world, by
his *pensar* whose ecstatic analogy is with music, fire, and lightning.
In his lecture on surrealism Paz had used lightning for the sudden
flash of poetic insight, and it occurs here: "No vimos sino el relámpago / No oímos sino el chocar de espadas de la luz" (we only saw
lightning / We only heard the light's clash of swords, *P*, 139).

In "Hermosura que vuelve" (Beauty that returns), a title referring
to the cyclical quality of beauty that can be reborn inside the poet,
the first stanza describes the unpredictable quality of beauty when
what is called reality is suddenly undermined:

El telón de este mundo se abre en dos.
Cesa la vieja oposición entre verdad y fábula,
Apariencia y realidad celebran al fin sus bodas,
Sobre las cenizas de las mentirosas evidencias
Se levanta una columna de seda y electricidad,
Un pausado chorro de belleza.
Tu sonríes, arma blanca a medias desenvainada.
(*P*, 144)

(The curtain of this world opens in two / The old opposition between
truth and fable ceases / Appearance and reality celebrate their wedding /
On the ashes of the lying evidences / A column of silk and electricity
rises / A slow jet of beauty / You smile, white weapon half unsheeted.)

Reality, lying evidences, turned to ashes (burned by the passion of
love) reveals (as in a theatre) its origins (cf. Breton's poem "Toujours
pour la première fois" (Always for the first time): "le rideau invis-
iblement soulevé / Rentrent en tumulte toutes les fleurs"—the curtain invisibly raised / The flowers enter tumultuously):[15] where
appearances are truth. Beauty becomes a weapon as well as a naked

body because beauty just is—"Tu nada más estás" (you are that's
all, *P*, 144)—and fights to deny the revenge of alienating reality.
Beauty shines like a star guiding man home. The poem ends (linking
star and muse and woman): "Nada más fulges, engastada en la noche"
(you only shine, set in the night, *P*, 144). The powerful verb *fulgir*
recalls the last line of Luis Cernuda's opening poem of *Los placeres
prohibidos* (Forbidden pleasures): "su fulgor puede destruir vuestro
mundo" (its brilliance can destroy your world).[16] The last line also
echoes Rubén Darío's sonnet "Venus" dedicated to the night star
and muse "como incrustado en ébano un dorado y divino jazmín"
(a golden and divine jasmin set in ebony), a line quoted by Paz in
his marvelous essay on Darío.[17]

"Estrella interior" (Inner star) expands on this notion of inner
beauty exploding ecstatically to reveal the ashes of reality as an inner
star inviting man to life: "Es una invitación a renacer porque cada
minuto podemos nacer a la nueva vida / Pero todos preferimos la
muerte" (it is an invitation to be reborn because each minute we
can be reborn to the new life / But we all prefer death, *P*, 146).
The Mexican's indifference to life, the living death of most urban
people: because they ignore the inner star. This star does not appear
in the latest fashions or on the general's lapel: it is invisible to those
in power. But it represents the "fresh water" that restores life's lost
harmony; that knocks down walls; that opens closed doors; that
fertilizes the desert. Without that water, without love the world is
a dead place:

> Todo cerrado impenetrable
> Todo daba la espalda
> Salían de sus cuevas los objetos horribles
> La mesa volvía a ser irremediablemente para siempre mesa
> Sillas las sillas
> Máscara el mundo máscara sin nadie atrás
>
>   (*P*, 148)

(Everything impenetrably closed / Everything turned its back / Horrible
objects came out of their holes / The table became irremediably forever a
table / Chairs chairs / The world a mask a mask with nobody behind it.)

But this moment of despair (the Sartrean thingness of the world)
can be redeemed by the inner adventure. The poem ends with the
world reborn:

Dejamos nuestros nombres a la orilla
Dejamos nuestra forma
Con los ojos cerrados cuerpo adentro
Bajo los arcos dobles de tus labios
No había luz no había sombra
Cada vez más hacia adentro
Como dos mares que se besan
Como dos noches penetrándose a tientas
Cada vez más hacia el fondo
En el negro velero embarcados

(P, 149)

(We leave our names on the shore / We leave our form / With our eyes closed into the body / Under the double arches of your lips / There was no light there was no shade / Each time further inside / Like two seas that kiss / Like two nights penetrating each other gropingly / Each time deeper in / Embarked in the black ship.)

The rotten selfish values of 1950s Mexico brushed aside: the couple plunge eyes shut into their inner voyage toward their depths, their truth; without name or form. This *fondo* (depth) is so easily ignored and substituted for history's illusory compensations (power, renown, privilege, politics). The black sailing ship, Rimbaud's *bateau ivre*, Baudelaire's *voyage*, [18] also evokes in its color the black word of poetry. Poetry releases inner freedom, innocence, Adam and Eve. Paz repeats his basic opposition in "Refranes" (Refrains): "Los días harapientos caen a nuestros pies / No hay nada sino dos seres desnudos y abrazados" (the ragged days fall to our feet / Nothing exists except two naked beings embracing each other, P, 150). The rags of history shed like clothes before making love: freedom is to lose your names and discover your anonymous universal being. And poetry is the only language capable of transmitting this in its archetypal, metaphorical mode. The last line of the poem "Semillas para un himno" catches this linguistic bliss: "Por un instante están los nombres habitados" (for an instant the names are inhabited, P, 152). Inhabited (with its Heideggerian echo) by real meaning, even if instantaneous, suggests that the lovers fall back into reality after.

The whole collection is a defense of poetry as a *relámpago* or illumination that once experienced becomes the only guide or torch to justify life in such a foul period of history as the 1950s in Mexico (in the world); it is a defense that does not stoop to the language of the enemy (prose) but is based on the metaphors that recall the origins reexperienced by the poet and lover.

El arco y la lira (1956)

Back in Mexico Paz reviewed the Mexican tradition in terms of his lucid and enthusiastic defense of poetry: his essays on López Velarde, Pellicer, and Gorostiza are part of his rescuing "poets" from the misreadings of history. His task was to upend the Mexican's "scorn" for the way he values his own literature (*Pe,* 66), especially in such a money-orientated culture as Mexico's. In 1954 he attacked the anthologist Castro Leal for a tepid, academic vision of Mexican poetry (when he collected this essay Paz censured much of his criticism) for poetry was a question of spiritual adventure, living out the poetic act. Paz sought to make poetry matter.

These ideas about poetry, dispersed in reviews, became the theme of one of Paz's most impressive books, *El arco y la lira*. This defense of poetry within the Mexican nationalistic context is daunting to summarize as the experience of reading it is part of its theme. Paz does not indulge in patient, analytical explorations of the history of poetry or the image or rhythm but offers sudden insights, partisan generalizations, sweeping views. It was primarily aimed at narrow-minded Mexicans, a *summum* of Paz's experiences in European literature. The opening paragraph, based on an attractive and hectic set of clichés about poetry, first sums up this dilemma for Paz and then states that these clichés are truths, but as generalizations have nothing to do with the experience of poetry. Because Paz argues from a subversive belief, his book is obsessive, pedagogically repetitive, passionate, and implicit in many poems.[19] To summarize this book would be to lift the ideas he attacks or defends out of this personal context (a surrealist poet returning to Mexico) to restore them to their abstract status. Paz's mode is deeply biased and suggestive; it cries out for polemic, to be argued with and contradicted. But few poets in Mexico were up to this task. The historical context and Paz's frenetic attempt to subvert the dominant ideology, then, create the tone. Like *Piedra de sol* (1957), *El arco y la lira* is a self-conscious attempt to synthesize a body of work. That Paz turned to prose, rather than his poems, typifies the climate of the times: prose was the language shared by the enemies, read by those who would not dream of reading a poem. Paz needed to carry his attack beyond the narrow confines of the poem. The book defends the poet as a subversive value ignored by those in power. The only certainty that Paz offers is the quality of his experience, the seriousness of his assertions, and the breadth of his readings. To refute the book would prove hard. For example, how would you argue with such a conviction as this?: "Poetry lives in the deepest layers of being, while ideologies and all that we call ideas and opinions constitute more superficial strata of our consciousness" (*A*, 40–41). If you share this personal belief, then Paz will confirm your own experience; if you do not, his language does not describe the experience that justifies the assertion (when religion or Marxism could be substituted for poetry). When Paz names the enemies of poetry—society divided into groups and classes or language deadened to cliché—does this imply that everybody is alienated, secretly looking for "poetry"? If only poetry can save man, yet so few read poetry, does not Paz's answer suggest a hermetic or initiate's insights? Could this explain his later fascination with Mallarmé? For Paz articulates how poetry could be at a general level and how absent it is in but a few isolated individuals who are the exception, our secret heroes. Paz's vision of the poet and change is aimed at the heretics, always a minority. An alternative reading would locate the above passage autobiographically: for Paz poetry had been his way out of the 1940s tunnel. When Paz writes: "The poem reveals to us what we are and invites us to be what we are" (*A*, 41), he must know that few ever discover their *ser:* that the context for Paz's passionately serious (a seriousness that links him with Breton) disquisition is an asphixiatingly alienated society. The density and richness of this book belies the fact that it is directed at deaf ears, at a majority too busy or too numb to care. Paz's real enemy is indifference. His overpowering manner, like a battering of the door, is a tacit recognition of this in Mexico of 1956.

For it is the poem that is Paz's real response: it is in the poem that language's full, plural, sensual nature is restored: "Thanks to poetry language reconquers its original state" (*A*, 47), not in prose, for prose is mutilation, alienation. Yet there are passages in the book when Paz breaks out of prose (cool, analytical discourse), passages that echo poems published elsewhere. For example, Paz describes the boil of language inside all of us: "Luminous creatures inhabit the thickets of speech. Creatures who, above all, are voracious. In the bosom *(seno)* of language there is a civil war without mercy. All against one. One against all. Enormous mass always in motion, engendering itself ceaselessly, drunk on itself. In children's, madmen's, cretins's, lovers's, or solitary people's lips images, word-play, expressions surging from nothingness, burst out. For an instant, they shine and flash" *(A, 35)*. Clearly not a fair-minded, quasiscientific description, but an outburst that succeeds in evoking the strangeness of inspiration (how words arise in the mind) within the poet. At this level and tone, this passage recalls his "Trabajos del poeta" in *¿Aguila o sol?* (1951). The last line recalls the last line of the poem "Semillas para un himno": "For an instant the names are inhabited" *(P, 152)*. When Paz describes the experience of love, the tide of love: "I touch your breasts, I brush your skin, I enter through your eyes. The world disappears. Now there is nothing, nobody. Things and their names and their numbers and their signs fall at our feet. Now we are naked of words. We have forgotten our names and our pronouns *(pronombres)* melt and bind together: I am you, you are I" *(A, 152)*; we can find almost identical passages in *Piedra de sol*. At times whether this is in prose or poetry does not seem to matter; it is the experience that justifies the language, the anger and enthusiasm. And it would be hard to deny that Paz succeeds with his words.

However, if we read *El arco y la lira* as autobiography that is impersonal, then we can accept that deeply held subjective experiences and beliefs form the basis of his arguments. The book becomes a vivid testimony to his experience of mid-twentieth-century history. For example: "Mysticism and poetry have lived a subsidiary, clandestine, and diminished life. The crushing has been unspeakable and constant. The consequences of poetry's exile are everyday more evident and terrifying: man has been expelled from the cosmic flow and from himself. But now nobody ignores that Western metaphysics ends in a solipsism. To break it, Hegel returns to Heraclitus. His attempt has not restored health. The rock-crystal castle of dialectics reveals itself at last as a labyrinth of mirrors. We must begin again" *(A, 101–2)*. This deeply felt paragraph could now be decoded: Paz, a quasi-mystical poet, suffered the agony of alienation, but found a way out of a sterile, rational, scientific civilization through a poetry that, like surrealism, wants to begin the cultural enterprise again, from the origins. Paz's title invokes this Heraclitean beginning, the necessity for poetry to be the mainstay of a society, not banished. Paz's "Hay que empezar de nuevo" (the last line) echoes a line from his 1955 "El cántaro roto": "Volver al punto de partida" (return to the starting point, *P*, 259) and is his remedy, the result of his soul-searching move away from revolutionary political thought to a poetic that was even more radical because it recovered the origins. Paz had experienced history as a dead-end, a prison (the rock-crystal labyrinth of mirrors emerged in his 1948 "El prisionero" concerning de Sade). Poetry had become the seed experience for a less horrific future because for rare but intense moments in his life as a poet, lover, and thinker Paz had felt the relief of a deeper, more anonymous, more liberating experience. Paz's truth can only be tested by experience.

Throughout *El arco y la lira* this personal basis becomes avoided, a form of reticence, but the dialectic between alienation and salvation oscillates rhythmically and constantly. Paz had called it *soledad* and *comunión* in 1945: it is the movement and theme of all his work, this book included. An example: "Poetry is metamorphosis, change, alchemical operation, and that is why it borders on magic, religion, and other attempts to transform man and make of 'this one' and 'that one,' this 'other' who is himself. The universe stops being a vast store of heterogeneous things. Stars, shoes, tears, trains, willows, women, dictionaries, all is one immense family, all communicates with itself and transforms itself ceaselessly, the same blood runs through all the forms and man can at last be his desire: himself" (*A*, 113). This passage could be a prose description of a poem from *Semillas para un himno*, a confession, a generalization about Western man, a metaphysical statement, a defense of poetry, but is primarily the rhythm of Paz's own experience.

At the same time as this personal level, *El arco y la lira* fascinatingly amalgamates Paz's readings: he combines lucid philosophical gleanings from Hegel, Marx, Nietszche, and Heiddeger with a great survey of visionary poets from the German romantics to Blake, Rimbaud, Eliot, and Breton, to anthropological insights from Frazer and Lévy-Bruhl, to writers like Otto, Jung, and many Eastern thinkers from Chuang-tse to Suzuki: all read and absorbed to give support to and confirm his own private experiences. Paz would rather move out into their experiences and presuppose a universal ahistorical collective experience akin to the mystic's than exploit the grain of his own. This is more than an act of humility, it is an act of solidarity with those who share what distinguishes Paz: a passionately felt lucidity.

In the last section of the book, "El verbo desencarnado" (The disencarnated verb), Paz deals with the social role of the poet as a revelation of his position in 1956. Paz's own tradition begins with the *poètes maudits*, those who have been exiled from the bourgeois order. The poet does not belong to this economic status and must earn his living another way. Paz associates the poet's rejection of these values with a revolutionary alternative that implies knowing his position. The poet's revolutionary aim would reveal "a man free of gods and masters, without intermediaries, faced with death and life" (an existential position). Thanks to his ancestors (Coleridge, Novalis, and particularly Blake) Paz can sketch out his program: "The poet wipes the sacred books clean of error and writes innocent there where we read sin, freedom where authority was written, instant where eternity had been engraved. Man is free, desire and imagination are his wings, the sky (heaven) is within reach of his hand and calls itself fruit, flower, cloud, woman, act" (*A*, 238). There is no need to read the Mexican specifics into this (authority = political caciques; eternity = the catholic church), for Paz views the poet (himself) as a teacher: his decree is to do with the inner life and how to lead a full life. The act (the last word of "Himno entre ruinas" of 1948) continues Paz's revolutionary belief that "poetry enters into action." Paz unites himself with the German romantics and the surrealists in protest "against the spiritual sterility of the geometric mind" (*A*, 245) that he had encountered in Europe and that he had blamed for destroying Europe. The last pages of the book give away Paz's 1956 stance, for it is a defense of surrealism, especially the postwar emphasis on "inner search" for an authentic self. At this level *El arco y la lira* glosses "El cántaro roto."

The book received intelligent responses, especially from Tomás Segovia and Manuel Durán,[20] and this was followed when Roger Munier translated it into French (1965) and later when it appeared in English (1973; cf. Helen Vendler).[21] From the acceptance of this book (1956) Paz confirmed his status as a poet and thinker in Mexico. From 1956 he could no longer be *ninguneado*. Paz had returned home as a surrealist and silenced his critics. Perhaps the most telling detail concerns Munier's French translation that was read by Breton who quoted from Paz in the catalog for the eleventh surrealist exhibition in Paris (1970).[22]

Theater

For Paz poetry can happen in any genre, so he included his only incursion into theater in his *Poemas* (1979). He dedicated this one-act play, *La hija de Rappaccini* (Rappaccini's daughter, 1956), to the surrealist artist Leonora Carrington, who designed the sets. Based on a Hawthorne short story, the play is clearly symbolic, a dramatizing of the roles described in the Tarot cards interpreted by the messenger in the prologue, a universal situation, with the Mother and her enemies, the King or man of power, the learned or rational intellectual, troubadour, and lovers. The love affair between Juan and Beatriz, Rappaccini's daughter, takes place in a medicinal garden, a garden of evil. Juan tries to save Beatriz from her father (her breath is poisonous) and administers to her an antidote that will restore her "true nature," free her of science and her father and let her contact life again. She drinks this potion and falls into her soul and dies. The messenger tells the audience that this mysterious drama "is still taking place" (*P*, 307). Is there a moral? That science poisons love in an evil world? And that there must be an antidote? Love?

The play formed part of a cycle of plays called *Poesía en voz alta* which included Genet, Ionesco, Tardieu, Elena Garro, and Lorca. Critics attacked the series for being too heretic and surrealistic. Manuel Calvillo reviewed these criticisms and their banal labels and praised Paz for bringing "poetry" to the Mexican stage, though in 1963 Paz insisted that he had no intention of writing poetic drama, but creating mystery or ritual play on stage (*Pu*, 274).[23] For Paz this venture marked the beginning of a new experimental phase in Mexican drama. The intention matched what he did in *El arco y la lira:* opening the doors to the best European drama of the time.

What is essential is that Paz did not water down his poetry for the stage: his charged stage language mirrors his own poems. For example, when Beatriz drinks the potion to see whether she can be cured of her death-inducing breath: "Ya di el salto final, ya estoy en la otra orilla. Jardín de mi infancia, paraíso envenenado, árbol, hermano mío, hijo mío, mi único amante, mi único esposo, ¡ cúbreme, abrázame, quémame, disuelve mis huesos, disuelve mi memoria! Ya caigo, ¡caigo hacia dentro y no toco el fondo de mi alma!" (now I've taken the final leap, now I'm on the other shore. Garden of my infancy, poisoned paradise, tree, my brother, my son, my only lover, my only husband. Cover me, embrace me, burn me, dissolve my bones, dissolve my memory! Now I fall, I fall inside and do not touch the bottom of my soul!, *P, 306*). The language recalls some of the intense moments in *El arco y la lira* or "Caigo sin fin desde mi nacimiento / caigo en mi mismo sin tocar fondo" (I fall from my birth without end / I fall into myself without touching the bottom, *P, 276*), from *Piedra de sol* (1957).

Piedra de sol

In 1957 Paz published *Piedra de sol*, a long poem summarizing his experience up to then and exploiting a Mexican motif, the Aztec calendar stone that stands in the Museum of Anthropology and History in Mexico City. Paz incorporated this poem unchanged into *Libertad bajo palabra* (1960 and 1968). Five English translations exist and Péret translated it into French.[24] It has received detailed critical studies, noted in the bibliography. It is a difficult poem that demands a wide knowledge of history and poetry, but it is without footnotes. Behind its facade of Mexican motifs and individual experiences, the poem is deliberately universal, embodying in its careful structure a clash of values (history/poetry) that result in a series of epiphanies. As a poem it parallels *El arco y la lira*.

In its first edition of 300 copies Paz included a prologue (deleted until the 1979 *Poemas*) that sets the poem in a universal mold: a Mexican frame illustrating a rhythm that transcends Mexican history. Paz composed the poem in 584 hendecasyllables (six are repeated), without a full stop. The number 584 relates to a Mayan system and the cycle of the planet Venus (Quetzalcoatl) around the sun. The duality of this planet (morning/evening; phosphorus/Vesperus) reflects the "essential ambiguity of the cosmos" (*P, 675*). The Mexicans linked the ending of the 584 cycle with the ending of an epoch and the beginning of another (i.e., a metaphor of rebirth); Venus for the West was also a rebirth symbol, linked with the moon, the resurrection of nature, etc. Paz extends these mythical analogies to Taoism, Ishtar, and Aphrodite. However, this information is implicit in the poem, which conveys the experience of rebirth; its spiral structure leads to an ending (without a stop) that edges the reader back to the start. This structure is a metaphor of time: that fusion of history (the linear time of reading) and repetition (irruption of archetypes in the epiphanies); history undermined by ecstasy. The Gérard de Nerval epigraph stresses this fusion of the cyclical clock (thirteen returns and it is the first) to the actual experience of time as the present ("le seul moment") that can either occur as banality, monotony, and alienation or as presence, the *instante, dicha* (joy). The rhythm of history and of this reading (a satisfying fusion) is that inevitably one falls out of ecstasy into alienation, but can return (the metaphor of rebirth, hibernation) to ecstasy.

Further devices structure the poem's dense, allusive lines: the use of *voy* (I go) and *buscar* (to seek); the notion of the Quest like Quetzalcoatl's descent into the night; the poem as an insomniac's *vigilia* (this vigil continuing Paz's kind of meditation) that ends with the dawn sun, rebirth, and life. The poem echoes Sor Juana's *Primero sueño* (1692), substituting a rational poetic discourse for a journey through *duermevela* (half sleep); the idea of a journey through woman's body, close to Péret's *Je sublime* (and the piece quoted earlier from *El arco y la lira;*) the idea that the poem is a dispassionate autobiography (references to Paz's stay in the United States, Spain, Paris; his readings of literature, mythology, history) as well as being a generation's epitaph (those marked by the Spanish Civil War, World War II, etc.).

Paz described the central theme as the "recovery of the amorous instant as a recovery of true freedom" in similar terms to his chapter "The consagration of the instant" in *El arco y la lira.*[25] A freedom won from history, within the poem, within the consciousness of the poet, what Paz called the "correspondence of personal life, historical life, and cosmic life."[26] Finally, this is a love poem to woman (the other) in all her ambiguities and historical guises.

However, most importantly, Paz's structure is a temporal one, banishing the normal halts and breathing spaces. The poem must be read in a rush, paralleling the onrush of time and history. This movement (engraved in the Aztec calendar stone) creates the experience of the poem. Analytical breaks would falsify the experience of the poem as being a faithful metaphor of the suffering of history and potential liberation from its oppression. The reader becomes involved in this process. The poem remains sufficiently open (not

personal or private, tending to general senses expressed in language
at its most Platonic) to allow others to identify themselves with this
twentieth-century parable.

The opening (and closing) six lines set the tone for this human
drama by describing the world of nature without man, but rocked
by the rhythms (life/death, day/night) that make up all life:

> un sauce de cristal, un chopo de agua,
> un alto surtidor que el viento arquea,
> un árbol bien plantado mas danzante,
> un caminar de río que se curva,
> avanza, retrocede, da un rodeo
> y llega siempre. . . .
>
> (P, 259–60)

(a crystal willow, a water poplar, / a high fountain that the wind bends, /
a well planted tree that dances, / a flowing of river that curves, / advances,
retreats, a detour / and always arrives.)

The natural softness of willow is opposed to hard crystal, the poplar
to water, the planted tree to dancing. This is an image of integration,
of a world not alienated or contaminated. It is the paradise of
innocence that promises itself to man and to which he can return,
momentarily. Into this perfection, this visionary world, man, the
poet, and history intrude.

One level of the historical experience is personal: the poet as lost
in the labyrinth, forgetting his name, his purpose, asking himself
questions about the past in Christopher Street (Berkeley), the refor-
ma Carmen, Oaxaca (Mexico), the hotel Vernet (Paris), Bidart (India), Perote (Mexico)—distressing moments of anguish and isolation:

> nombres, sitios,
> calles y calles, rostros, plazas, calles,
> estaciones, un parque, cuartos solos,
> manchas en la pared, alguien se peina,
> alguien canta a mi lado, alguien se viste,
> cuartos, lugares, calles, nombres, cuartos. . . .
>
> (P, 268)

(names, sites, / streets and streets, faces, squares, streets, / stations, a
park, lonely rooms, / stains on the wall, somebody brushing his (or her)

hair, / somebody singing by my side, somebody getting dressed, / rooms, places, streets, names, rooms.)

A litany of senseless traveler's or exile's experiences, moving through streets and hotels into oblivion (who was that combing her hair?); but this snatch of despair cannot last (the rhythm of alienation/ ecstasy) and is immediately followed in the poem by a reference to Madrid, 1937, where the poet overcame the horrors of history through love: a love that defends and recovers paradise, roots, what is "invulnerable" to time: "no hay tú ni yo, mañana, ayer ni nombres, / verdad de dos en sólo un cuerpo y alma, / oh ser total" (there is no you nor I, tomorrow, yesterday or names, / truth of two in one body and soul / oh total being, *P*, 269). Love with the other (woman) draws out man's fugitive essence; the lovers's dualities fused in one body and mind, echoing the subversive Rimbaud's ideal "To possess the truth in one soul and body."[27] Paz has given a literary connotation to ecstasy, hoping that naming it will convey it, but it does not. What it does point out is the idea of this love-experience as an alternative to history.

From this recovery of total being the poem immediately crashes back into alienation: "cuartos a la deriva" (rooms adrift, *P*, 269) and another ferocious litany of what divides man from man and man from himself:

> y las leyes comidas de ratones,
> las rejas de los bancos y las cárceles,
> las rejas de papel, las alambradas,
> los timbres y las púas y los pinchos,
> el sermón monocorde de las armas,
> el escorpión meloso y con bonete,
> el tigre con chistera, presidente
> del Club Vegetariano y la Cruz Roja. . . .
>
> *(P, 270)*

(and the laws food for mice, / the bars of the banks and prisons / the bars of paper, barbedwire fences, / bells, barbs, and spikes / the monochord sermon of arms / the cloying scorpion with hat / the tiger with top hat, president / of the Vegetarian Club and Red Cross.)

The monsters in society seem to emerge from a medieval bestiary. The general ideas (i.e., concentration camp or bank and capitalism) are localized by qualities (the bars of banks, writing paper, and prisons): the rotten masks that degrade society. These enemies of man collapse when two lovers make love and recover (in a lovely phrase): "el olvidado asombro de estar vivos" (the forgotten astonishment of feeling alive, P, 271), where *estar* carries the impermanent, existentialist sense.[28] Love has become a "combatir" (combat): it changes the world more effectively than revolutionary politics ("si dos se besan / el mundo cambia,"—if two kiss / the world changes, P, 271); love makes the wine taste of wine, water of water, bread of bread; it restores sensual contact with the world (cf. "Himno entre ruinas"); it opens doors, humanizes people, releases man from his faceless masters: "el mundo cambia / si dos se miran y se reconocen, / amar es desnudarse de los nombres" (the world changes / if two look and recognize each other, / to love is to strip naked of names, P, 271). Rimbaud's *changer la vie* (to change life)[29] moves from poetry to Paz's ideal of love as antidote to spiritual death. As a love poem these lines also evoke Pedro Salinas, particularly his line "vivir en los pronombres" (to live in the pronouns).[30] For love allows the lovers to recognize his (or her) true nature, which is freedom from contingency and nightmare. Paz continues with another list: rather than resign yourself to history and societal values better a whore (like Eloise) and not "ceder a las leyes" (give in to the laws, P, 271) like Abelard and be castrated. Paz romantically considers any rebellion better than none: "mejor el crimen, / los amantes suicidas, el incesto" (better crime, / suicidal lovers, incest, P, 271).

Paz veers from this rebellion to the nightmare of history in another angry list that begins with the origins of recorded history in Homer, through Socrates's Greece to Ninevah, the Romans (Brutus), the Aztecs (Moctezuma), Robespierre, Churruca (the battle of Trafalgar), Lincoln, Trotsky (murdered in Mexico), and Madero, all victims of a life "ajena y no vivida, apenas nuestra" (somebody else's and not lived, hardly ours, P, 275). Because of these victims the poet seeks true life, beyond the given, beyond history: "la vida es otra, siempre allá, más lejos" (life is other, always beyond, further away, P, 275), following Breton's "L'existence est ailleurs" (Existence is somewhere else).[31]

If love is redemption from the hell of history, then for the male poet, woman is both muse and carnal lover: the other that completes his divided, solitary self. Many sections of the poem convey this woman, the poem a lyrical tribute to "her" as a generic woman, a feminine principle, a word, a memory that comes alive in the poem itself, in the mental life of the poet, then reader. At night the poet slips into her body (she could be lying asleep at the insomniac poet's side; she could be poetry as a quest towards self-awareness; she could be his own liberated thoughts);

> voy por tu cuerpo como por el mundo,
> tu vientre es una plaza soleada,
> tus pechos dos iglesias donde oficia
> la sangre sus misterios paralelos. . . .
>
> (P, 261)

(I go through your body as through the world, / your belly is a sunny square, / your breasts two churches where blood / officiates its parallel mysteries.)

Lovely, visual lines dealing sensually with awe, like the Song of Songs. This passive woman then becomes a mythological figure, a Venus, a Mexican fertility goddess (cf. "Dama Huasteca"):

> tu falda de maíz ondula y canta,
> tu falda de cristal, tu falda de agua,
> tus labios, tus cabellos, tus miradas,
> toda la noche llueves, todo el día
> abres mi pecho con tus dedos de agua. . . .
>
> (P, 261)

(your maize skirt sways and sings, / your crystal skirt, your water skirt, / your lips, hair, look, / all night you rain, all day / you open my chest with your water fingers.)

This woman is the poet's internalized muse or anima: she is identity, a mediatrix that redeems man from his male isolation. Behind the individuality of a woman lies an archetype: "entrevista muchacha reclinada / en los balcones verdes de la lluvia, / adolescente rostro innumerable" (half-seen girl reclining / on the green balconies of rain, / innumerable adolescent face, P, 263). The reader might want more concrete details about these girls, but Paz seeks to locate what exists outside the accidents of history:

he olvidado tu nombre, Melusina,
Laura, Isabel, Perséfona, María,
tienes todos los rostros y ninguno,
eres todas las horas y ninguna,
te pareces al árbol y a la nube,
eres todos los pájaros y un astro. . . .
(P, 263)

(I have forgotten your name, Mélusine, / Laura, Isabel, Persephone, Mary, /
you are all faces and none, / you are all hours and none, / you are like the
tree and cloud, / you are all the birds and a star.)

She is cosmic (outside the hours) and natural; she survives the cor-
rosion of history. The names listed derive from myths and famous
literary muses (Petrarch, Garcilaso). This list returns later in the
poem: "Eloísa, Perséfona, María, / muestra tu rostro al fin para que
vea / mi cara verdadera, la del otro" (Eloise, Persephone, Mary, /
show your face so that you may at last see / my true face, the other's,
P, 276). Only woman can restore the poet's true face by opposing
her radical otherness to him; only she can wake him up from the
nightmare: "despiértame, ya nazco" (wake me up, now I am being
born, P, 276). For the female archetype (though Paz avoids Jungian
language) embodies the ambiguity of life itself, like Kali:

vida y muerte
pactan en ti, señora de la noche,
torre de claridad, reina del alba,
virgen lunar, madre del agua madre. . . .
(P, 276)

(life and death / pact in you, lady of the night / tower of clarity, queen
of dawn, / lunar virgin, mother of mother water.)

Kali, Coatlicue, Venus, Aphrodite, Ishtar: she can gather up man's
fragments, tie up his broken bones, restore life to him. Woman is
"puerta del ser" (door to being, that is a mental door and a vagina);
through that door the poet will see (the verb ver, to see, used twice)
a world of harmonious, life-enhancing communion: "todo se co-
munica y transfigura" (all communicates with itself and transfigures,
P, 277). This is the promised paradise enjoyed by lovers, whose
bliss augurs a world where all will be lovers and poets: "adonde yo

soy tú somos nosotros, / al reino de pronombres enlazados" (where I am you we are us / to the kingdom of linked pronouns, *P*, 277), again evoking Pedro Salinas. For the third time *despertar* (to wake up) is used, associating this with *El laberinto de la soledad*. Once awake the poet faces his being given qualities of a life of archetypal solidities: sea, bread, rock, source, spring (*P*, 277) dissolving the poet in the anonymous depths of his freedom: "indecible presencia de presencias" (unsayable presence of presences, *P*, 277), where the crucial word is *indecible*. The poem can only lead the reader like the words lead the poet to the edge of the precipice.

The woman who best illustrates woman as waker-up and restorer of being and her precarious position in history is Mélusine. She occurs twice, half woman, half serpent, well known in French mythology. She is a water nymph who leads a human life but is spied on during her Saturday transformation and is lost:

> yo vi tu atroz escama,
> Melusina, brillar verdosa al alba,
> dormías enroscada entre las sábanas
> y al despertar gritaste como un pájaro
> y caíste sin fin, quebrada y blanca,
> nada quedó de ti sino tu grito. . . .
> (*P*, 267)

(I saw your atrocious scale, / Melusine shine green at dawn, / you slept curled up in the sheets / and on waking you screamed like a bird / and fell without end, broken and white, / nothing left of you but your scream.)

This woman, all women, degraded by man; all that is left is this victim's scream. Paz brought Mélusine into his poem while in Mexico because Mélusine had fascinated Breton in *Nadja* (1927) and especially *Arcane 17* (1947). Paz deliberately quotes from Breton: "Mélusine aprés le cri, Mélusine au-dessous du buste, je vois miroiter ses écailles dans le ciel . . ." (Mélusine after the scream, Mélusine above the bust, I see her scales flash in the sky).[32] Paz secretly affirms his surrealist heritage in the Mexico of the 1950s. José Emilio Pacheco felt that *Piedra de sol* could not have been written "without the experience of surrealism."[33]

But fascinating and subtle as Paz's dramatic clash between history and poetry might be within the poem, as a poem *Piedra de sol* must work lyrically at a more intense level than simply "expanding consciousness." And it does for some of the individual lines are staggering: "los tigres beben sueño en esos ojos" (tigers drink dream in those eyes, P, 261) or: "sobre mis huesos llueves, en mi pecho / hunde raíces de agua un árbol líquido" (you rain on my bones, in my chest / you sink roots of water, liquid tree, P, 261) or: "cabelleras de arañas en tumulto" (head of hair of spiders in riot, P, 262) or: "lates como una ardilla entre mis manos" (you beat like a squirrel in my hands, P, 272) or: "oí cantar mi sangre encarcelada" (I heard my imprisoned blood sing, P, 277).

In the 1950s cold war in ideologically rigid Mexico, Paz's long poem argued that the world can change (through carnal love), that rebirth is the individual's contribution to the revolution ("Everyday is to be born," P, 276) and, most delightfully, that being alive is what counts. Paz had combined an intensely felt lyrical poem in a suggestive structure with a deeply felt metaphysics. In 1970 Pacheco still thought it Paz's masterpiece.[34]

In 1958 Paz collected poems written in cities round the world—Mutra, Tokyo, Venice—in *La estación violenta*, whose title symbolized "passion and reason, action and reflection."[35] He viewed the book as an autumnal harvest. In 1960 he collected most of his previous work in *Libertad bajo palabra*, which repeated his 1949 title (like Cernuda kept *La realidad y el deseo* for all his successive editions). There is a definite sense in these collections of the end of a phase.

Salamandra

In 1959 Paz returned to Paris as a diplomat, and from 1962 to 1968 went to India as Mexican ambassador—in all a stay of nine years abroad. Paz caught his Parisian years in *Salamandra* (Salamander, 1962), a transitional book, moving away from the long lines of his 1950s poetry. From the 1960s Paz began to collect nearly everything that he wrote in prose—essays, prologues, reviews, obituaries—suggesting that prose had become as crucial as poetry in his attack on history.

In a series *Corriente alterna* (Alternating current; collected in 1966 under that title) Paz, in 1960, wrote on Henri Michaux, eroticism, de Sade, and others, essays that revealed that his attitude to what he had defined as evil remained constant. He does not avoid his European debts, telling Luis Suárez (1959) that the world was planetary and so was culture and that a Mexican could not afford to

ignore this fact.[36] He outlined his fears of the advance of technology
and its insidious erosion of inner values, the "immense conformism"
of the urbanized masses.[37] But there is still a sense of the lonely
prophet in Paz. In 1961 Pacheco stated that *Libertad bajo palabra*
had appeared in silence and that Paz had been *ninguneado*.[38] In 1962
Paz still insisted on the artist's freedom from all societies, capitalist
or communist, as an *inconforme*, a critic. Prose came to the forefront
as Paz defined his role as a critic who must criticize the language
of the enemy. He wrote (1961): "Today history does not only occupy
the whole terrestrial space but also invades our thoughts, empties
our secret dreams, pulls us out from our houses and throws us into
public emptiness" (*Pu*, 67).

Salamandra's break with *Libertad bajo palabra* concerns the presentation and typography of the poem. Paz has moved to a more
ascetic and spatial poetry built up with single words and short
phrases floating in white spaces. He had been reading Mallarmé
and Apollinaire (translating both carefully, with notes). They lead
him to conceive of the poem as a visual as well as oral object,
suppressing punctuation. Paz shifts to individual words and wordplay (as Alejandra Pizarnik noted)[39] in order to increase his use of
silence, the white spaces locating meaning between the lines, in the
wordless mind. Equally Mallarmean, poetry had become the critique
of language itself within the poem, for the enemy had corrupted
the poet's secret dreams, his thougths. History had shrunk to language and corrupted it, an *escritura gangrenada* (gangrened writing,
P, 317). The poet's Mallarmean task was to give a purer sense to
the tribe's words. You feel that Paz reads dictionaries to find words
not contaminated by use. In the middle of a poem, without any
reason, the word "alabastro" (alabaster) appeared (*P*, 333), for a
moment innocent of history (though it occurs in Darío's "El reino
interior"—the inner kingdom—that Paz had been reading at the
time as he has a poem dedicated to Darío).[40]

Many of the poems in *Salamandra* are circumstantial (i.e., to
Reverdy on his death) and many are based on reading. (Quevedo,
Tablada, Cernuda, Darío); with some short lyrics close to the spirit
of haiku that Paz had started to write as early as 1955 (cf. *Piedras
sueltas* / Loose stones [*P*, 153–159]) on his return from Japan. But
behind these poems there is a sense of a pattern: many of the poems
were written at night, during the poet's vigil or insomnia (perhaps
because the day was given to diplomatic work) where the poet's

thoughts cluster around his writer's table and his light (this *lámpara,* a Mallarmean symbol of the writer's cool-headed retreat into his privacy) with a sleeping or remembered woman/muse nearby and the hostile city outside. The City (Paris, Mexico City, London) continues to be his T. S. Eliot emblem for evil, rationality, soulless work, masses, rootlessness. Many of these poems evoke despair and futility, but the best are still imbued with erotic qualities that begin at the level of words and rise to poems about woman and love as his antidote and self-therapy. The poems become more counterpointed, self-dialogues dramatizing history and poetry.

From early on Paz had created a personal myth around the word: the opening poem of *A la orilla del mundo* (1942), "Palabra" (Word), a *conceptista* play with ambivalent language, based on dualities but seeking a Word that transcended these dualities. The slightly later "Las palabras" (*P,* 69) deals more aggressively with the poet's matter: words are whores that must be whipped, dried, stepped on. In 1942 reviewing Moreno Villa's poems *La noche del verbo,* Paz equates poetry with words (in the plural), not necessarily beautiful or sonorous but significant ones.[41] In 1949 the prose poem "Libertad bajo palabra" (that later became the prologue and gave its name to the collection *Libertad bajo palabra* and remained as prologue to *Poemas,* 17–18) suggests a hunt for a single word, but shows that the poet still works with words, hordes of words, seeking *la Palabra,* the ideal, mental, inexpressible word like the mystic's *ay.* The 1949 section "Trabajos del poeta" dramatizes the poet's grapple wtih words. Only in the 1960s does the poet start focusing on single words and short lines rather than words, phrases, images, and long lines. In "Disparo" (Firing) one word leaps up like a horse, "la palabra que revienta las palabras" (the word that smashes the words, *P,* 320) and that wakes him up to say *acuérdate* (remember).

The opening poem of *Salamandra* "Entrada en materia" (Entry to matter) suggests the poet plunging Neruda-like (cf. Neruda's "Entrada a la madera" [Entry to wood] of *Residencia en la tierra* [1935] where *madera* becomes *materia*)[42] into the matter/mother of language in search of spiritual health. The actual state of language mirrors the fallen world because language names it and brings it into focus and consciousness; consequently, it is *algarabías* (gibberish), senseless language, noisy world. This *algarabía* is also the City with its neon lights, its spiritual death, its cars, headlights, and bones (*P,* 311). But somewhere in this hell there is a space for "el sagrario del cuerpo / el arca del espíritu" (the sacrarium of the body / the chest of the spirit, *P, 311, 315*); the chest where words are kept intact. This poem hints at a need for initiates, for hiding words in secret places from the vulgar—what Breton had suggested surrealism do, go underground.[43] Because language reflects the corrupt world, it is an invisible tide, a pollution, an evil. And this evil has permeated with its clock (time) into sexuality and mind, into the very "quicios del lenguaje" (hinges of language).[44] The poem vividly describes this state of corruption.

The moon, the very emblem of poetry, has been degraded by the world:

> La luna
> Como un borracho cae de bruces
> Los perros callejeros
> mondan el hueso de la luna
> Pasa un convoy de camiones
> sobre los cuerpos de la luna
> Un gato cruza el puente de la luna
> Los carniceros se lavan las manos
> en el agua de la luna
> La ciudad se extravía por sus callejas.
>
> (*P, 313*)

(The moon / like a drunkard falls flat / The street dogs / strip the bone of the moon bare / a convoy of lorries pass / over the bodies of the moon / A cat crosses the bridge of the moon / The butchers wash their hands / in the water of the moon / The city gets lost in its alleys.)

Paz weaves together the defiling of the moon and poetry (with Li Po's suicide suggested) with the foul city, in abrupt words and short phrases that gain in sound.

The poem then moves to the isolated poet at his table, tortured by his *"conciencia"* (consciousness, *P, 313*), listening to his thoughts as they are exteriorized on to the white paper as this poem. He tries to interpret what his thought is saying but cannot. The poem has become an analogy of the chaotic city: arthritic Spanish, a skyscraper of words, babel (*P, 314*). The poet victimized by other people's words, his own words "hinchadas de razones enemigas" (swollen with enemy reasons, *P, 314*). By the end of the poem the poet discovers his strategy of reclaiming the dead words from the dead

city: "Yo he de decir lo que no dicen / Yo he de decir lo que dicen"
(I must say what they do not say / I must say what they say, *P*,
315). By increasing the worlds's promiscuity, their erotic charge
(Breton: words make love)[45] words will recover their spiritual vitality
and thus restore the poet's divided self.

Many poems in *Salamandra* trap this despair that all language
belongs to the city: "Repeticiones" (Repetitions) and "Augurios"
(Auguries; cf. Blake's "Auguries of innocence") are lively examples.
The short poem "Aquí" (Here; it is chapter 149 of Julio Cortázar's
Rayuela [Hopscotch, 1963]) captures the city as a nightmare labyrinth, with the poet as empty as *niebla* (mist). The poem "Peatón"
(Pedestrian) mocks the bourgeois for not missing poetry in his city
life. It situates a nameless person in the boulevard Sebasto, self-
absorbedly strolling but who looks up to see

> un pescado volaba.
> Cambió el semáforo hacia el verde
> Se preguntó al cruzar la calle
> en qué estaba pensando.
> (*P*, 321)

(a fish flew past / The traffic lights changed to green / He asked himself
as he crossed the street / what he was thinking about.)

The isolation of the poet in the City characterizes the poem titled
"Luis Cernuda" (in 1979 it became an obituary with his dates added).
Cernuda epitomizes all poets in his lost room, in his immaculate
clothes, in a hostile city: "escribe el poeta las palabras prohibidas /
signos entrelazados en una página" (the poet writes the prohibited
words / signs linked together on a page, *P*, 324). Although the
specific references to Cernuda are obvious (his dandy clothes, his
isolation, his surrealistic collection *Los placeres prohibidos*, [1931]) he
becomes here an example. Only in this secret room can true liberation happen, the truth "burning on decrepit walls." This poet's
truth has nothing to do with public works nor moral guide lines
but is born in silence and contemplated silently. It is only at this
private task that the poet can restore language as a "transparent"
bridge between his inner desire and enemy reality. Transparency (a
crucial term for Paz from the 1960s on, partially derived from Breton
and Mallarmé)[46] becomes a synonym for purity, absence of distortion

and a restoration of the word/thing gap; no more alienated words, the poet names reality. Paz stresses the secret quality of this operation. The poem "El tiempo mismo" (Time itself; by 1979 Paz altered this to "El mismo tiempo" [The same time]) ends by proclaiming this desired state of "transparency" (*P*, 336) following a long meandering meditation on time, identity and language. It opens with the familiar dilemma: the lost city, which is seeking some meaning, forces the poet into the anguish of uncertainty: "está vivo en mitad de la noche / habla para oírse" (he is alive in the middle of the night / he speaks to hear himself, *P*, 331). The poet knows that a *presencia*, a full-lived time, exists to justify the fragmentation of city life; that the fig-tree of his childhood will return and liberate him (this belief is the poet's act of faith) and that the poem is a *vaivén* (an oscillation) between moments of time and vision of which one is a blackbird standing on a grey stone in the city (*P*, 335). The poet senses this other time and longs for the relief of this pure present: "sin horas ni peso ni sombra / sin pasado o futuro / sólo vivo" (without hours nor weight nor shadow / without past or future / just alive, *P*, 336). The poet's message: how to become alive in the city of the dead (Mexico City, Paris). Many poems depict this skill—"Vaivén" (Oscillation) or "Interior"—where this moment of coming alive is due to an erotic encounter. "Alba última" (Last dawn), a love poem, explicitly catches the lovers's eternity of now while the hostile city outside awaits: "Afuera pasa un taxi / con su carga de espectros" (outside a taxi passes / with its load of ghosts, *P*, 375). The experience of the bliss of now, pure time, renders the notion of a tomorrow meaningless. The poem ends on an ironic question: "¿Mañana será otro día?" (Will tomorrow be another day?, *P*, 375).

The short poem "Palpar" (To caress), which first appeared in French in 1959 in a *Lexique succint de l'érotisme* as part of the surrealist exhibition in Paris,[47] recounts, as the infinitive of its sensual verb implies, the fullness of this now but in terms of plurality: the poet restores his lover's other bodies, her totality of selves and meanings; just as he does this with words liberated on a page. The true body is many bodies:

> Mis manos
> abren las cortinas de tu ser
> te visten con otra desnudez

descubren los cuerpos de tu cuerpo
Mis manos
inventan otro cuerpo a tu cuerpo
(*P*, 360–61)

(My hands / open the curtains of your being / dress you in another nakedness / Discover the bodies of your body / My hands / invent another
body for your body.)

The poet and lover are united by their hands (to caress, to write)
and in their sensuality and imagination as the way to the plural
movement of truth.

The title poem "Salamandra" takes on the enemy of science (European rationality; linear fixed-meaning, literal language). When
Paz reads this poem on record, another voice counterpoints the text
(in the poem it's the use of brackets).[48] This counterpoint opposes
the dead natural-history taxonomy (salamander, a suarian, lives in
cracks) with the living depth-associations of the poet: the salamander
as an emblem, like D. H. Lawrence's phoenix, of passionate life (as
it is in Yves Bonnefoy's poem "Lieu de la salamandre" [Place of the
salamander] and "La Salamandre" [1953]).[49] This conflict recalls
the old romantic opposition between poetry and science, life and
death. Paz summarised his attitude in a play of words: "Inocencia
y no ciencia" (innocence and not science, *P*, 327). When the poet
(not the scientist) meditates on the salamander, he explores a tissue
of vital resonances: the first concerns one of the four elements (ancient, sensual science), fire. The salamander represents an antidote
to the abstract city's vertiginous geometries (*P*, 377), its chimera
and thirst. The poet links the salamander with the sun, its "roja
escritura / en la pared de sal" (red writing / on the salt wall, *P*,
377) punning the *sal*amander (salt), then with a star, a lost girl,
and a buried seed. The poet opens out latent associations; he liberates
the word salamander. It is made to stand for the origins embedded
in the dead layers of history: "grano de energía / dormida en la
medula del granito / Salamandra / niña dinamitera" (grain of energy /
asleep in the core of granite / Salamander / dynamiter girl, *P*, 377–
78).

As the poet exposes these forgotten associations so does the salamander come alive and remind the poet of his mythic origins: it
speaks like a *"fuente"* (fountain), a *"herida"* (wound) and bursts into

his mind like an *"espiga"* (ear of corn, *P,* 378). The poet then associates this salamander with air, an exclamation, praise, and a girl in purple stockings running through a wood. This taciturn animal becomes heraldic and has little to do with its biological or evolutionary functions. The salamander, like the phoenix, survives death, becomes what transcends history, the *"eje"* (axis, *P,* 379). In spite of the scientist's interventions in brackets, the poet then hunts out the Mexican associations with Xolotl the two-headed dog that accompanied Quetzalcoatl through the underworld seeking out the bones of the dead. The axolotl-salamander becomes analogy, the poet fertilized into discovering through images the origin inside himself (ironically narrated in Julio Cortázar's short story "Axolotl"):[50]

> Salamandra
> dardo solar
> lámpara de la luna
> columna del mediodía
> nombre de mujer
> balanza de la noche
> (*P,* 380)

(Salamandra / solar dart / Moon lamp / column of midday / name of woman / balance of night.)

The salamander fuses the four elements (earth, fire, water, wind); becomes the salt of life; the origins now remembered by the poet, "roja palabra del principio" (red word of the beginning), *P,* 381). But the poet must guess for its reality: "Es inasible Es indecible" (Its ungraspable Its unsayable, *P,* 381) and be reborn through passion and patience. There are clear alchemical connotations in this process of transformation. This is the poet's arduous labor: to patiently and solitarily subvert the deadly discourse of science until the very word itself reveals its truth: man can recoup his roots and thus liberate himself from the tyranny of history: the poem ends: "Salamadre   Aguamadre" (saltmother   Watermother, *P,* 381). Through inspired wordplay—in an erotic ritual of letting the words copulate—the poet realizes that *madra* becomes *madre* and *sal* (salt water), *agua* (sweet water). This mother water, the origins, suggests a fertilized poet. Only love precipitates this process of alchemical purification. In 1962 Paz defined the salamander as an "erotic symbol"; man is amphibious, has two selves, moves between two elements (water and air; history and poetry), like the salamander.⁵¹

During his years in Paris (1959–62) Paz came to envision poetry as criticism of language. "Salamandra" criticizes a worn-out word and rediscovers its latent possibilities (origins, myths, xolotl, mother, salt, water) and this rediscovery is the poet's liberation from how history has contaminated his mind's language. The poet's task is to break up language in order to cure it (and this again recalls Henri Michaux): "sonaja de semillas semánticas" (P, 386). Like a shaman the poet shakes this rattle of potent syllable seeds to inaugurate a new language, a new music that will exorcize the *sombras* (shades) of science, the cities, the twentieth-century ideologies and dogmas.

Chapter Four

India, the Far East, and Return to Mexico

Mallarmé

Octavio Paz's six years in Asia (1962–68) can be seen as a series of journeys with cultural clashes between Mexico, Asia, and Europe taking place inside the poet as well as years of meditating on love, reading, and poetry, experiences collected as poems in *Ladera este* (Eastern slope, 1969) and as prose in *Puertas al campo* (Doors to the field, 1966), *Corriente alterna,* (1967), and *Los signos en rotación* (Rotating signs, 1965)—with monographs on Lévi-Strauss (1967), Duchamp (1968), and eroticism (1969); it is a prolific output. In his prose Paz sought to communicate his enthusiasms, readings, and perceptions in an accessible medium. In the poetry, the tendencies noted in *Salamandra* coalesced to become counterpoint meditations on language, memory, love, and poetry itself. The process of writing became his theme as if the poet could no longer afford the luxury of unconscious innocence so deeply had the rot of history rooted itself inside him. Behind this profusion of writing lies one constant: Paz's reading of Mallarmé and Buddhism.

In 1967, showing his copy of Mallarmé's *Un coup de dés . . .* (Dice throw) to Laus, Paz said: "I read it continuously."[1] And his long poem *Blanco* shows the effects of this reading for Mallarmé shares an epigraph with Tantric Buddhism. Both Mallarmé and Buddhism posit the negation of the ego of the writer or adept. Mallarmé/Buddhism argues that the poet disappears in his poem, absorbed into the social medium of language. This ascetic process becomes an ethical stance, as if the poet's ego is where history has set up its citadel. Mallarmé called this the "disparition élocutoire du poète, qui cède l'initiative aux mots" (the elocutory disappearance of the poet who cedes the initiative to words):[2] the poet's liberation is the extinction of his personality in the T. S. Eliot sense, as the words in the poem take on their own life. As a metaphor of the

107

process of writing—words freed from conventional associations, syntaxes—this phrase from Mallarmé is a fine description. For Paz this was more than an ethical position, though it was the beginning: "the moral of the writer does not lie in his themes nor in his principles but in his conduct faced with language" (*A, 72*). For Paz this became his practice, a kind of mental hygiene.

In *Los signos en rotación*, which became the epilogue to the second edition of *El arco y la lira* (1967), Paz opened by evoking Lautréamont's dictum about the future poetic society.[3] Whether this belief was still practicable was for Paz the question facing poets and revolutionaries. His own belief in this necessary society was *irrenunciable* (unrenounceable).[4] Paz's problem in the mid 1960s was how to work toward this society. He had characterized his epoch as having lost its world image, swamped by the universal vocabulary of technology, in a crisis of meaning. This critical discussion of technology (another term for history) lead Paz to reaffirm his anguish that "la verdadera vida" (true life, *Si, 33*) was still missing. Man in the 1960s was still lost among meaningless things and trapped in circular thought. And here Mallarmé offered the best solution. In evoking Mallarmé, one should remember that poetry for Paz was a metaphor of a liberating process that far exceeded verse. So Mallarmé's break with linear succession, the tyranny of typography, in favor of spaces and page whiteness is a metaphor of a release. Mallarmé had turned poetry into a critical act (against language as it is used in society), negating the possibility of poetry as a final polished statement by replacing it with the poetic act, the process where there are no final solutions. The axis word for Paz is *tal vez* (perhaps). Paz reduced the Mallarmean position to a process where the poet's verbal imagination shrinks reality to its idea, a word on a page; this in turn is reduced to an "infinite probability" when approached as a word (the word is not the thing). The poem then becomes closed to the alienating world, but open to nameless white space as a liberation from fixed meanings where the poet or reader's fantasy/desires/imaginations flow. For Paz, updating this conjuring trick, starts his poetics with this loss of the world image (i.e., an alienated world fixed in an alienated discourse) and forces the poet to find reality inside himself. But still crucially, continuing his link with Breton's surrealism, this mental language then liberates the poet by creating his otherness. From Mallarmé Paz adopted the visual impact of enigmatic signs that need to be deciphered by an initiate, thus elbowing out the enemy, where a poem becomes a musical score. Another liberating adoption: language has become interiorized, taking on its own reality, without needing to designate or be a symbol of exterior reality. For a poet this suggests a powerfully subversive role in society: to create an inner language with a minimum of referentiality, undermining the realistic illusion of prose, like music whose essence is its temporal flow. Paz incorporated most of his gleanings from Mallarmé into *Blanco*. His knowledge of Mallarmé and Mallarmé criticism lead to his translation of the enigmatic "Sonnet en ix" in 1968, collected with his notes in *El signo y el garabato* (The sign and the scrawl, 1973).

Blanco

Blanco borrows much from Mallarmé's intentions, from its title ("Les blancs en effet, assument l'importance, frappent d'abord").[5] The first edition was a scroll without pagination but folded and packed into a box or hard folder; 550 copies were printed, with a warning to the reader—describing Paz's own intentions—that has not been incorporated into later editions. Paz briefly noted six alternative readings that his typographical experimentations offered: there are four different print faces in two different colors with different columns, lost in later editions. This original visual impact was part of its Mallarmean reading where the poem should start off being as illegible but as beautiful as a musical score.[6]

The epigraphs from the Hevajra Tantra and from Mallarmé's "Sonnet en ix" act as signposts for an interpretation. From Tantra, Paz borrows the idea of the scroll and ritualized copulation *(maithuna)*, but none of the dogma. Despite its self-consciously difficult structure, *Blanco* is a marvelous love-poem to the woman's white body, analogous to the white page on whose flesh/body/paper the poet writes his fleeting but intense desires. Apart from the Mallarmean implications of the temporal/spatial form, this poem is very Pazian.

Paz had fixed six readings: but this itself is a metaphor for the startling fact that there are no longer shared fixed meanings in the world of the 1960s. Freedom has now become the poet's consciousness of this multiplicity of choices and meanings, only limited by time. The white space (and target) visually symbolizes the infinite Mallarmean possibilities inherent in words, like the white space at the center of a mandala. In a sense Mallarmé's preface to *Un coup de dés* functions as a gloss to Paz's structure: the spatial clusters of words and phrases without punctuation, with large white margins, act to accelerate or slow down the movement where this way of writing mirrors the movement of reality itself. That is, the reader creates the structure, itself grounded in time, coming alive in the actual moment of reading. And reading is primarily a sensual experience (spaces, colors, typography, and words as sounds before meanings); as Mallarmé stated: "Je suis arrivé à l'idée de l'univers par la seule sensation" (I arrived at the idea of the universe solely by sensation).[7] This sensuality, close to nonreferential music, functions as Paz's Mallarmean metaphysics: a thinking embedded in the ecstasy of copulation, of copulating words, metaphors of liberation. The act of reading (reacting to words through liberated senses) doubles the act of writing: both are processes (actions, events) in time toward an understanding that never actually happens on the page, only in the mind. This Paz calls *inminencia* (imminence, *P, 490*) while Mallarmé can only say about this experience: "L'homme poursuit noir sur blanc" (man chases black on white);[8] this pursuit of black words toward understanding is like listening to a concert where the only possible understanding is the now of the listening. Paz called this a poem.

Paz turned to the heretical Tantric tradition because Mallarmé lacked the realization that his words set free on a white page were erotic symbols, that words set free magnetically attract and repel each other. A missing epigraph could have been Breton's "les mots font l'amour" (already cited). Tantra sacrilizes what should be the central ritual in all societies: the ecstasy of copulating lovers. The analogy between writing and making love becomes the heart of this poem. In the text the sign "woman" is fused with *la palabra* (the word as feminine), with the poet as their lover. And the word need not refer to a real woman out there, for another ghostly title for *Blanco* could have been "rotating signs," where the movement of words interacting within the text is erotic, and self-knowledge (liberation) results from the sensation of these rotating signs, of the words liberated from their duty to represent fixed meanings.

As Paz wrote, the reading of *Blanco* is generated by the poem itself. Of course, this is an ideal and the reader is not obliged to follow these instructions; the poem can seem to be overloaded with pious, Mallarmean intentions. But letting the words free (by introducing novel combinations) does give the reader more participation. The ideal remains faithful to his previous writings: language sets free its multiple associations, its othernesses as the poem sets free the *otra* (woman, anima, muse) within the poet: that is, inner freedom of "la mirada" (the inner glance) over *lo mirado* (what is looked at, exterior reality, *P, 496*).

Paz shifted the Mallarmean initiate's play with words and white spaces toward pleasure and eroticism and ritualized copulation, celebrating woman, not as a symbol or word, but as a reality. Paz does not exclude reality, for there is a reference to a *nim* tree (*P, 494*) under which he and Marie-José got married in 1964. In this sense, this poem is more lyrically conventional than it seemed: it celebrates the poet's new love.

The poem opens, self-conscious of its being a poem opening: "el comienzo / el cimiento / la simiente / latente" (the beginning / the foundation / the seed / latent, *P, 485*), where through rich sounds the wordplay, like bells, releases overlapping meanings: analogies of the origins, the seed, sperm, the latent poem (liberating mental experience) that this poem is pursuing. The poem sets up the innocent, ageless, self-aware, promiscuous words before language-use (history) defiles it. The poem then situates the poet poised by his Mallarmean lamp, at night—"late una lámpara" (the lamp beats, *P, 486*), where its light symbolizes the poet's illuminated wakefulness. Two pages of imagistic play with "lamp" (now a sign, a word on the page) follow: it is a survivor, "something" rises up its stalk to explode in clarity (i.e., its light bulb), it's a head on a pike, a sunflower, a flower. "Lamp" has liberated the poet's wordplay. The sign "lamp" links *Blanco* back to *Salamandra*. Mallarmé's *lampe* occurs in "Brise marine" (Marine breeze) where the *lampe* (the poet's night light) becomes transformed through a pun into a *palme* (a palm tree), itself a metaphor of the poet's transforming ability; the poet is not a slave of reality.[9] Paz echoes this conceit with his "lámpara / palma" in *Blanco* (*P, 486*).

Following *lámpara's* opening out into analogies, there is a double column, bringing in the love/passion element: the naked nameless girl by the fire, with the poet's sensations spreading up into "la noche magnética" (magnetic night; an allusion to Breton, *P, 487*).[10] The poem then moves back to its single spinal column where the electrical charge bringing clarity in to a light becomes an analogy for language's energy rising up toward clarity: "un presentimiento de lenguaje" (a presentiment of language, *P,* 487). The poet, like the traveler Livingstone (whom Paz had been reading at the time), waits, in his case for inspiration in a sterile world. Livingstone's *patience patience* recalls Mallarmé's advice about how to work as a poet: "avec une patience d'Alchimiste" (with an alchemist's patience).[11] The poet compares himself to a desert, a dried-up, dusty Mexico; gagged. The wait for language has become an "expiation" (of rotten clichés). To speak in the twentieth century is to polish bones (the dead bones of used-up words) but this must be done to achieve the liberation of transparency.

The next section is double columned, returning to the love poem. The poet enters "her," the her (muse, other) inside himself, created by his desire. Inside himself, with her, the poet finds the truth of water "en un lecho de vértigo" (in a bed of vertigo, *P,* 489). All that remains of this "país de latidos" (country of heart beats, *P,* 486) where lovers find themselves is *transparencia:* words at one with the white page and where the poet sees reality, his othernesses, without the distorting medium of language.

The single column returns to evoke the desert, dead language, spikes, thorns, and vultures. But a rhythm of expectation is building up (drums, heart-beat). The poet beats the drum of language and earth's belly trembles, releasing the green word. For Paz the birth of the word in the poet is given natural, spontaneous connotations.

The poem again changes to a double column where the two columns join or copulate, imitating a Tantric text where columns open and close like legs.[12] Here the poet penetrates the naked erotic woman (the poet fertilizes words). From this liberated words bubble up (like sperm or seed). The single column that returns now calligramatically describes the stalk up which words arrive (like sap or electricity), and the poet at last sees his own thoughts inside himself (as he exteriorizes them on to the page), like "un archipiélago de signos" (*P,* 491; cf. *Si,* 41), for his thoughts are diaphanous: "no pienso, veo" (I do not think, I see, *P,* 491). His liberation is to find himself in the inner white space of the mind.

The next copulating double column illustrates the poet's fall into himself down to his origins, into the sexualized archetypes that generate real meaning:

yedra abórea lengua tizón de frescura *el firmamento es macho y hembra*
temblor de tierra de tu grupa *testigos los testículos solares*
lluvia de tus talones en mi espalda *falo el pensar y vulva la palabra*
(*P*, 492–93)

(tree ivy brand of freshness *the firmament is male and female* / earthquake of
your buttocks *witnesses the solar testicles* / rain of your heel on my back
phallus the thinking vulva the word.)

This is a mock return to the cosmic procreation of life, as the birth
of the word inside the poet, not visible to anyone but for the poet
an ecstatic experience where the poet, in Mallarmé's words, under-
goes "la joie de contempler l'Éternité, et d'en jouir, vivant, en soi"
(the joy of contemplating Eternity and enjoying it in him, alive).[13]
The act where real language is born is the lover's cry of pleasure:
"caer en tu grito contigo" (to fall into your scream with you, *P*,
493).

This new poetics liberates the poet from the pressures of his age:
"La irrealidad de lo mirado / da realidad a la mirada" (the unreality
of what is looked at / gives reality to the looking, *P*, 493). For
reality lies in the mind, but the mind's reality dissolves language,
thought, and culture and can then perceive the world as it is and
was from the start. The poet becomes a poet as he writes and chases
meaning. Mallarmé: "Devant le papier, l'artiste se fait" (In front of
the paper the artist makes himself).[14]

The poem ends on one last long column. The poet finds himself
at his fluid center, thought and words in movement like music (*P*,
494). The drought is over, the night flows, music flows, woman
flows. *Fluir* (to flow) is a metaphor of time and liberation. In this
state language is magnetized: "jazmín y ala de cuervo / tamborino
y *sitar* / No y Sí" (jasmin and crow's wing / small drum and *sitar* /
No and Yes, *P*, 494–95), where the copulative "and" joins the
fragmented *jazmín* with the crow's wing, not normally relatable but
here liberated from their isolation. The analogy that joins things is
love: "dos sílabas enamoradas" (two syllables in love, *P*, 495). All
is harmonious, one: body/world/spirit, for transparency (the mental
experience of liberation from opacity) abolishes all differences. It
was man with his words who brought in categories and judgments.
The poet has discovered pure language: "Estás desnuda / como una

sílaba" (you are naked like a syllable, *P*, 496). Music floods all as
the lovers' bodies *derramar* (melt away). The poet has gained *la
mirada*, (insight).

Paz found Mallarmé liberating; he borrowed insights and found
much common ground, especially in the idea that language makes
the poet (nòt the other way round) and that words have flesh like
a woman. Awakening the reality of these living carnal words inside
the sterile, numbed poet became Paz's task, his antidote to his age
and expiation of it in him. The poem achieves this with its profusion
of allusions to the five senses, to music, to erotic rhythms.

Lévi-Strauss and Eroticism

In *Blanco* Paz exaggerated his belief in inner freedom to the point
of identifying with Mallarmé's ideal of keeping intruders out. Paz's
attempt could have roots in the fact of living culturally and lin-
guistically isolated from his Mexican/European roots or the result
of his own happiness and second marriage. But this retreat inside,
away from history and into the mysteries and thrills of the creative
process, became the theme of much of his poetry's strange literal
realism: about the poet himself in front of a white sheet of paper,
making himself. But Mallarmé's intention of escaping his times was
more radical than Paz's: "Je vais me cloîtrer en moi" (I am going
to cloister myself in myself).[15] If Paz followed suite, it was only
for a brief while. The poems of *Ladera este* (1966) and *Vuelta* (Return,
1976) move outward, again to grapple explicitly within the poem
with the enemy. But in his prolific prose works of this period Paz
does not retreat into his mind.

In the mid-1960s Claude Lévi-Strauss's works on the universal
structures of myths and mind had broken out of anthropological
specializations and fascinated many literary intellectuals. Paz re-
sponded publicly with *Claude Lévi-Strauss o el nuevo festín de Esopo*
(Claude Lévi-Strauss or Aesop's new Feast, 1967), taking on one of
the key intellectuals of the times (Paz has done the same with Sartre,
but never head-on in one book), both critically and exegetically,
reading Lévi-Strauss from the point of view of a poet.

Paz discovered in Lévi-Strauss an antihistorical bias where myth
is studied as a universal mental operation that is natural and unconscious, not a historical projection. Paz laconically illustrates his
agreement with references to linguistics, de Saussure, Marxism,

Sartre, and Buddhism. He acutely analyzes Lévi-Strauss's appeal and his literary style, which he compares to Bergson, Proust, and Breton (in whose work analysis and intuition subtly blend). However, Paz did not simply write an exegesis of a fashionable thinker. In his "Intermedio discordante" (Discordant interval) he accuses Lévi-Strauss of ignoring poetry—Dante, Baudelaire, Coleridge—and for classifying poetry, painting, and dance as inferior to music: "I confess that I cannot understand his impatience with poetry and with poets."[16] Paz then argues that poetry is an equal mental activity to myth and music, for all transmute time into a special nonhistorical experience in the present as a *presencia;* a negation of temporality. So Lévi-Strauss represents the scientific world that is hostile to poetry; Paz revenges himself against Lévi-Strauss's "philosophical bad temper" (*Cl,* 70) by comparing his thrill of reading as poems both *Le cru et le cuit* and Mallarmé's *Un coup de dés.* This little expository book, which also defended poetry eruditely and passionately, was quickly translated into English (1972) and French (1970) and reviewed acutely by anthropologists like Edmund Leach.[17]

Conjunciones y disyunciones (Conjunctions and Disjunctions, 1969), a title that describes a methodology of arguing through opposites that Paz has made his own from Lévi-Strauss, leads into a book dense with quirky perceptions about Buddhism and Christianity, the body sign, metaphors, Tantra, and Taoism—especially the opening with his *cara/culo* (face/backside) metaphorical opposition studied in a Posada print and a Quevedo poem. The book, an intellectual tour de force, based on Paz's readings in Tantra, de Sade, Bataille, and N. O. Brown, is framed by a very 1960s preoccupation, what Paz calls the rebellion of the body; otherwise Paz prolongs his *francotirador* (sharpshooter) battle with repressive history.

Paz again studies ways of resolving the *yo/otro* (I/other) duality that historical conditions have imposed; one example was the Baudelairian *carcajada* (roar of laughter), a metaphor of pleasure, a throwback to an earlier stage in history, the unity of the origins. Paz continues to define life's rhythms as a continual possibility of a return to a nondualistic experience: "In this sense our condition is not historical."[18] This rhythm has remained constant over 8,000 years of social relationships, but Paz now calls it the clash between the reality and pleasure principles (from Freud via Brown, replacing his solitude/communion terms of the 1950s). Paz's key metaphor for the pleasure principle is *cuerpo* (body). In poetry language restores this body, through the poem's appeals to the senses. But due to historical circumstances, this return can only flourish subversively, during a magical *instante*, in societies that are by nature repressive, like the Mexican (*Co, 27*).

Paz excitingly discusses the sign "sex": the anarchic, subversive sexual drive that "lacks a name and a class" (*Co, 28*), which Marxism ignores, for it is such a deep, nonhistorical drive that the experience of sexuality posits a golden age (*Co, 28*). Paz analyzes capitalism along N. O. Brown's lines (gold/excrement; rational economics/anal retention)[19] to argue that man's liberty lies in not allowing his dualism ever to congeal into one half: the deadening nonbody sign. Paz appeals for a continual oscillation, for that is life (*Co, 43*); the dialogue between body and nonbody "is man" (*Co, 62*). For brief moments, as in Tantra's ritualized copulation *maithuna*, man can recover his crushed otherness (his feminine side in the case of a man) in the act of love (*Co, 79*), as exemplified in *Blanco*.

Basic to Paz's delirious speculations is his critique of Western erotics (symptomized by de Sade): the belief in rationality, progress, history, and revolution has lead to the dead end of "tortures" (on the other, not love) and isolated "orgasms" (sexuality, not eroticism), never liberation (*Co, 117*). Then Paz returns to his lifelong crusade: only art rebels against Western discord—what he labels the rebellion of the senses (*Co, 125*), linking Novalis, Rimbaud, and the surrealists.

Paz summarizes the alienated quality in Western life by absences of "images, symbols, rituals. Imaginary forms that are nevertheless real due to our desires and obsessions; ceremonies in which images at last take on body without ceasing to be images" (*Co, 126*), for what is real is desire, the mind. Paz offers an anthropological critique of the Western void, the imageless world without ceremonies or rituals to sacralize human experience. But Paz also indicts Stalin and official Marxisms as equally to blame for his period's "infernal" view of man. Paz's book ends as another manifesto of his beliefs: art as the only truly revolutionary activity that wants to change life, for only passion can recover a "magnetic" reality. Paz felt that the 1960s youth movement reverted to surrealist values (spontaneity, enthusiasm) that heralded a "passionate, vital, libertarian heresy" (*Co, 137*).

From India in 1968 Paz reaffirmed his poetics of the ecstatic "now," while rejecting the eternities of all religions and political dogmas. His study ends by citing Breton's surrealist values—based on love, poetry, and liberty—as the only way to undermine "our abject world" and wake up to the values condensed in words like *presencia* and *amor*.[20]

Ladera este

The reality of Paz's years in India and of his readings there deliberately invade nearly all the poems of *Ladera este* as the circumstantial supports that allow the poems to transcend themselves as history. The strangeness of the Indian context, its exotic appeals, explains the density of Paz's notes at the end, though the same strangeness contributes to the poetry. *Ladera este* balances lyrical poems of an erudite traveler with lengthier, heavier poems invoking Paz's already elaborated vision. At the end, Paz reedited *Blanco*. In essence, *Ladera este* is one long love-song to Paz's second wife and to women in general.

The formal technique and typography follow directly from *Salamandra*, with similar visual impacts of lines floating in white space and no punctuation. Reading the poems produces a staccato effect as if each line is a unit or musical note in a score, though often lines continue syntactically into the next. These poems convey a fluidity, a movement of life analogous to fleeting impressions. Over this period Paz came more and more to view the poem as word-sensations that are mental images and thus echoes, shadows, nothing (close to Reverdy). This inner dissolving art in the mind, Paz calls a "spiritual exercise" (*C*, 71).

The first section, "Ladera este," includes travel poems built up on vivid impressions, perceptions, and ironic contrasts, often spiraling into meditations on art. The poet holds his Mexico in mind as he wanders across the Indian subcontinent, leaving a trail of place names along his poems: Udaipur, Mysore, Utacamud, and Herat. A typical poem would be the emblematic "La higuera" (fig-tree), almost a natural historical description of a fig-tree with the poem referring vividly to an actual tree. Many of these poems are slight and deal in colors, sensations, and movement—intense visual details similar to Carlos Pellicer. The second section, "Hacia el comienzo" (Toward the beginning), contains celebratory love poems.

The opening poem, "El balcón" (The balcony), sets the scene as a night time insomniac's meditations from a balcony overlooking New Delhi. The summer heat, insect noise, a sense of exile, and

strangeness are vividly portrayed: "un cuerpo fofo el aire / un ser
promiscuo sin cara" (the air a porous body / a promiscuous being
without a face *P*, 394). As well as seeing India, the poet recalls
Ustica (its name deleted) where he once had a vision of true life
(recounted in "Ústica" in *Salamandra*).[21] The poet drifts back to the
present: "Estoy aquí" (I am here, *P*, 394) and describes the clouds
and moon. Leaning on his balcony, he surveys the odd city of New
Delhi:

> las piñas de hombres y bestias por el suelo
> y la maraña de sus sueños enlazados
> Vieja Delhi fétida Delhi
> callejas y plazuelas y mezquitas
> como un cuerpo acuchillado
>   (*P*, 395–96)

(the clusters of men and beasts on the ground / and the tangle of their
linked dreams / Old Delhi rank Delhi / alleys and small squares and
mosques / like a knifed body.)

The poet penetrates the city in powerful images; but behind this
India lies mythic India whispering "remember" (*P*, 396). The poet
then returns to his predicament in time, as if waiting for something.

Meditations about the nature of time and identity cut across many
poems. "Perpetua encarnada" (Everlasting incarnate; in a note Paz
calls it a plant that symbolizes poetry [*P*, 684]) sets its reality in
the heat of the day and the relentless sunlight of India in an exuberant
garden full of fruit and flowers. The poet notices a lizard fixed in
place not time (unlike man). The poet "from his now" (*P*, 409),
conscious of his temporality, seeks to be permanent like the lizard
or the leaves. But man is different:

> Estoy atado al tiempo
>   prendido prendado
> estoy enamorado de este mundo
> ando a tientas en mí mismo extraviado
> pido entereza pido desprendimiento
> abrir los ojos
>   evidencias ilesas
> entre las claridades que se anulan.
>   (*P*, 410)

(I am tied to time / caught enchanted / I am in love with this world / I grope about in myself lost / I demand integrity I demand detachment / to open my eyes / untouched evidences / between the clarities that annul themselves.)

Then the poet spies the plant of the title, its everlasting leaves poetry itself. Language and consciousness—"razón del hombre" (reason of man, *P,* 410)—separate him from nature by giving him the sense of time's transience. Living this transience fully is liberating. The poem ends: "veo oigo respiro / Pido ser obediente a este día y esta noche" (I see hear breath / I ask to be obedient to this day and this night, *P,* 410). The pure present-tense verbs of the senses, the rich but simple "this" (the here and now) differentiate the poet from the lizard.

Life experienced from this rich temporal transience is what Paz calls the vision: seeing reality—its relation with the subject—as it is. "Felicidad en Herat" (Happiness in Herat), dedicated to Carlos Pellicer (written in June 1963) explores this open-eyed vision. The poet visits a mosque and some tombs. At dawn he sees colors and birds and hears water—a reality as insubstantial as his own thoughts. In a hotel room he suffers the cold wind of history. Then, without preconceived plans, in the garden of the Ladies, he climbs up the turquoise dome of a minaret, and it happened:

> No tuve la vision sin imágenes,
> no vi girar las formas hasta desvanecerse
> en claridad inmóvil,
> el ser ya sin sustancia del sufí.
> No bebí plenitud en el vacío
> ni vi las treinta y dos señales
> del Bodisatva cuerpo de diamante.
> (*P,* 419)

(I did not have a vision without images, / I did not see the forms spin until they vanished / in immobile clarity, / I did not drink plenitude in emptiness / nor saw the thirty-two signs / of the Bodisatva diamond body.)

The string of negatives separate the poet from orthodox religious illumination, whether sufi or Buddhistic. He rejects this immobile, timeless, imageless *vajra* perfection. He continues:

Vi un cielo azul y todos los azules,
del blanco al verde
todo el abanico de los álamos
y sobre el pino, más aire que pájaro,
el mirlo blanquinegro.

(P, 419)

(I saw a blue sky and all the blues, / from white to green / all the fan of the poplars / and on a pine more air than bird / the whitish black blackbird.)

This vision of a blackbird on a pine is so direct and childlike that it excludes everything else. The poem ends by interpreting this vision: "Vi las apariencias. / Y llamé a esa media hora: / Perfección de lo Finito" (I saw the appearances. / I called this half hour: / Perfection of Finiteness, P, 419). This poet's perfection is to live his finiteness, his temporality, and not to deny it; there are no hidden realities, only superficial ones grasped by the senses in love with the works of time, the appearances of this world. This is more than simply looking at trees and a blackbird; it is looking at them for the first time, as miracles in themselves. Breton's "L'Oeil existe à l'état sauvage" (The eye exists in a wild state)[22] is the surrealist vision; eyes rinsed of prejudices, culture, and language. "Domingo en la isla de Elefanta" (Sunday on Elefanta Island) offers the same open-eyed vision: a love poem about the poet's wife that ends by rejecting Shiva and Parvati (archetypal Indian lovers):

nada les pedimos, nada
que sea del otro mundo:
sólo
la luz sobre el mar,
la luz descalza sobre el mar y la tierra dormidos.

(P, 470)

(we ask them nothing, nothing / from another world: / only / light on the sea / barefooted light on sea and earth asleep.)

No otherworldly visions occur but sunlight on the sea,[23] barefooted light fusing land and sea in a cosmic repose of sated lovers.

The poems that meditate on language and reading—"Lectura de John Cage" (Reading John Cage), "Tumba del poeta" (Poet's tomb), "Carta a León Felipe" (Letter to León Felipe)—share this intention to restore the primacy of the senses: "recobrar la ignorancia / saber del saber" (to recover ignorance / knowledge of knowledge, *P*, 436): the wisdom the poet seeks is to cast off erudition, his culture, his responsibilities and plunge back into the world without categories, names, or anything that fixes the vertigo of movement which is life. In "Soltura" (Fluency): "Las cosas se desataban de sus nombres / al borde de mi cuerpo / yo fluía / entre los elementos desceñidos" (Things untied themselves from their names / at the edge of my body / I flowed / amongst the loosened elements, *P*, 439). Outside repressive, value-laden, categorizing language, outside his body (in his liberated mind) the poet flows in the bliss of elementary existence, casting off history.

"Vrindaban" subtly ties together these notions.[24] This long poem sets up its scene with the poet writing (writing about writing) at night in India. The speed of his thoughts is compared with the racing of a car, counterpointed throughout this hectic, breathless poem. The poet's thoughts rush back in time to memories of adolescence, and return to the now of writing under his night lamp while words and phrases rush through his mind. He sees again in imagination India's ruins, stink, and beggars, the fever of its daily life as rich as a peacock's tail (*P*, 423). Images rise and vanish in this mental race—in a kind of frantic music. The poem seeks the poem, trying to light the poet's way:

> Escribo sin conocer el desenlace
> de lo que escribo
>   Busco entre líneas
> Mi imagen es la lámpara
>   encendida
>   en mitad de la noche
>   (*P*, 423)

(I write without knowing the outcome / of what I write / I seek between lines / my image is the lamp / lit / in the middle of the night.)

In his mind's eye an Indian Sadhu stares at him like a saint or an animal. The poet tried to talk but "me respondió con borborigmos" (he answered with borborigms, *P*, 424); but the Sadhu, perhaps illuminated, had retreated inside himself. The poet then races out of this memory back to his primary analogy (car/thoughts) then back

again to this perplexing saint. The poet intuitively rejects this kind
of inner salvation; locked out of life, the Sadhu is an *ídolo podrido*
(a rotten idol, *P,* 425). But this saint aids the poet to define his
position:

> Yo estoy en la hora inestable
> El coche corre entre las casas
> Yo escribo a la luz de una lámpara
> Los absolutos las eternidades
> y sus aledaños
>   no son mi tema
> Tengo hambre de vida y también de morir
> Sé lo que creo y lo escribo
> Advenimiento del instante
>
>   (*P,* 425–26)

(I am in the unstable hour / The car races between houses / I write by a
lamp's light / Absolutes eternities / and their outskirts / are not my theme /
I am hungry for life and also for dying / I know what I believe and I write
it / Advent of the instant.)

The poet delights in existentialist life; the moment enriched by the
threat of death. This act of living in time sculpts and undoes in its
rhythms "el ser entero" (entire being, *P,* 426). The poet glories in
his consciousness of this state, grabbing time (*P,* 426). The poet
assumes his personal history, memory, and otherness: "Hablo siempre
contigo / Hablas siempre conmigo / A obscuras voy y planto signos"
(*P,* 426, I talk always with you / You talk always with me / Obscurely I go and plant signs). This is the poet's credo, refined by
his stay in India: to move with time into the dark but exciting
future (more nows), writing poems (sign/seed/plant) that will fer-
tilize and liberate his readers.

The second section's opening poem "Viento entero" (Entire
Wind)[25] recreates this exciting, liberating perpetual present as the
clime where lovers live: the poem begins in an Indian bazaar; the
poet's mind then flashes back to Paris and a girl. The poet shifts
to the present in a weaving that is the movement of consciousness,
and reverts back to his naked lover eating a peach. He then jumps
to Santo Domingo and the United States invasion (1965), to a garden
planted by Tupu Sultan, to revolutionary Mexico and back again
to the "muchacha real" (real girl, *P,* 453). The poet is awake and

alive to this everchanging present; reality cleansed by the wind, the world "transparent" (*P*, 453). He then leaps back to his muse: "Tus ojos se abren y se cierran / animales fosforescentes" (your eyes open and close / phosphorescent animals, *P*, 454) and continues to laud his lover in analogies with landscape and sea. He is diverted by a memory about a saint's tomb and a youth who gave his lover a grenadine, by Amu-Darya and then Indian night falls with the woman still there like a mental image inside the poet: "Oigo tu latir en la sombra" (I hear your heart beat in the shade, *P*, 455) and the lovers act out the archetypes Shiva and Parvati. The poet then swerves back to Lahor, to some trees and light, and on to his infancy, Mexican landscapes, his Mixcoac fig-tree. She, his muse, is now inside the poet. The poem ends with dawn breaking over the fulfilled lovers: "No pesan más que el alba nuestros cuerpos / tendidos" (not weighing more than dawn our bodies / lying down, *P*, 457). In this poem the speed of the analogies and associations is matched by that of the reading to give an image of the awakened, fertilized other-communicating mind.

All the love poems invoke this inner world of mental images, where the writing, and then reading, of the poem become a spiritual exercise slowly derealizing the world as designated by words to restore the fuller meanings inside the mind: "Nos volvemos inmensos / sólo por conocernos / con los ojos cerrados" (we become immense / only by knowing each other / with our eyes closed, *P*, 458). Once the poet has seen through dead language, he sees reality: "El mundo es verdadero / Veo / habito una transparencia" (the world is true / I see / I inhabit a transparency, *P*, 459) where words and mind are transparent and transparency is a metaphor of immediacy, not alienation.

"Maithuna" (Tantric ritualized copulation) comprises several fragments invoking lovemaking, naked lovers, and bodies. Some of these read like drafts for *Blanco*, with columns and individual words like gasps or shouts. Another love poem, "La llave de agua" (Water key), conveys the poet's baptism, his discovery of water-inspiration through his lovers. It ends: "Esa noche mojé mis manos en tus pechos" (that night I wet my hands in your breasts, *P*, 466) where "hands" unites poet who writes and lover who caresses.

The second section of *Ladera este* ends with "Cuento de dos jardines" (Story of two gardens), another long poem transmitting "la vivacidad de uno de esos momentos" (the vivacity of one of those moments, *P*, 470). The poet meditates on places: his Mixcoac childhood garden, his grandfather, the totemic fig-tree. From India he evokes his past in Mexico, the Mexico of "El cántaro roto." The poet conjures up another garden in India with its *nim* tree so real that "se oía el jadeo de las raíces" (you heard the panting of its roots, *P*, 473). Then, from a meditation on this *nim* tree where he had learned how to reconcile himself with everchanging movement, he met a *muchacha* (a girl, *P*, 474) who became his lover during a monsoon season. Together they set off, she an *Almendrita* (*P*, 475), real India, mother truth, in her vagina. The poet then extolls her archetypal virtues and they get married under the *nim* tree, at one with time and life: "transcurrir es suficiente" (to pass with time is sufficient, *P*, 476). They lived in their garden with cats, crows, and other Indian birds. The poem changes back to the *ahora* (now)— out of sacred memory—to a ship journey and an albatross off Durban. The poet wonders what has happened to his garden, and answers: "No hay más jardines que los que llevamos dentro" (there are no more gardens than those we carry inside, *P*, 477). As the lovers flow on with time, experiencing bliss, the poet defines this life: "Pasión es tránsito: / la otra orilla está aquí" (Passion is passage: / the other shore is here, *P*, 477). On board ship the poet forgets all his book learning, his explorations of Hindu and Buddhist philosophies, because physical love teaches more:

> Olvidé a Nagarjuna y a Dharmakirti
> en tus pechos,
> en tu grito los encontré,
> *Maithuna,*
> dos en uno,
> uno en todo
> todo en nada,
> *¡sunyata,*
> plenitud vacía,
> vacuidad redonda como tu grupa!
> (*P*, 477–78)

(I forgot Nagarjuna and Dharmakirti / in your breasts / in your scream I found them, / *Maithuna* / two in one, / one in all / all in nothing, / *sunyata,* / empty plenitude / emptiness round as your buttocks.)

The lover's *grupa* is richer and wiser than all the concepts of Oriental philosophy; the poet has found the erotic source of all thinking about life. On board the ship, all the poet's Asian experiences are converted into memories as "cristalizaciones casi mentales" (almost mental cristalizations, *P,* 478), with the poet firm in his belief in the relief of the now: "Los signos se borran: / yo miro la claridad" (the signs are wiped out: / I look at clarity, *P,* 478).

Politics and 1968

In October 1968 Paz resigned as Mexican ambassador in protest against the Mexican government-supported massacre of some 340 students in the Plaza de Tres Culturas, Tlatelolco, just before hosting the Olympic games. He called 1968 a turning point in Mexican history—as it was in his own life. From 1968 to today (1985) Paz has led an itinerant life based in Mexico City but teaching abroad, mainly in the United States (Harvard), receiving many honors and prizes and editing *Plural* (1971–76) and *Vuelta* (1976–), both outstanding literary magazines.

In 1968 Paz had been invited to participate in cultural events celebrating the Olympics but, disgusted by the massacre, he wrote a brief angry poem and thus enmeshed himself with contemporary history. "México: Olimpiada de 1968" (*P,* 429) was Paz's formal condemnation of political dirty-handedness. The act of writing about the lack of *limpidez* (limpidity) suggests that Paz was assuming public responsibility for his own moral stance. The poem yokes the stain of blood with a moral flaw in Mexican politics and the poet's anger and shame. In 1970 Paz published *Posdata* (a postscript to *El laberinto de la soledad*) which polemically explored further this student massacre. It became a best-seller, reaching fourteen editions by 1980. It was attacked from every conceivable angle as frivolous, tasteless, antisocialist, and anti-Mexican. Carlos Fuentes called it an "uncomfortable book," while Paz was quite aware that "my words will irritate many people."[26]

Paz's argumentative note sets the book's tone: for him the Mexican is a history, not an essence. The duty of the intellectual is to criticize the masks this "history" adopts, for criticism is an attempt to liberate the Mexican from the paralysis of the past into action, akin to psychoanalysis. From this date Paz begins to write politically, not invoking the values of poetry but defending democracy. His critical assault on history does not end as a defense of poetry. In *Posdata*

Paz lucidly analyzes the student movements of the 1960s in terms of alienation from technology, the constitutional disease in all societies (*Pos*, 26). He carries over from *Conjunciones y disyunciones* his invocation of the now of pleasure obscured by the idea of progress and history. Man is a "being who desires" (*Pos*, 27), not one who works. But Paz moves from this surrealist position to link Mexican and East European students: both demand democracy. Paz draws similarities between the Mexican and Russian postrevolutionary systems, sharing bureaucracies and a special political rhetoric. Paz's historical explanation for this comparison is that Mexico is still dominated by its Aztec past. The student massacre was an expiation ritual, for the past is still alive. Paz then moves on to analyze the absence of democracy in Mexico as a critique of power. The veneration of the president, the "sacred horror" to intellectual dissidence (*Pos*, 54), the two Mexicos, the other Mexico, the politician's "asphyxiating rhetoric" deepen his earlier attacks on Mexican nationalism. His role as a writer is to purge this moral gangrene from language. At the end Paz denies that Mexico is ripe for another revolution. In the Mexico of the late 1960s—radical student politics and ideological nationalism—Paz's little book was attacked more than any previously.

Over the next decade Paz used his own magazines to further his defense of democracy, continuing to attack Russia and its allies Cuba and Nicaragua, and creating more enemies in the process. He collected these articles in *El ogro filantrópico: historia y politica 1971–1978* (The philanthropic ogre: history and politics 1971–1978) and *Tiempo nublado* (Cloudy weather, 1984). At times the insistence and intensity of Paz's public fight for his ideal of a plural society alternative to both West and East recalls the moral passion he had located in Breton, who exemplified the notion that the poet must act in the historical arena "against morality, the powers and social institutions" (*O*, 7). In many ways Paz also recalls Camus's similarly unpopular position with *L'Homme revolte;* Camus is one of Paz's few "uncorruptibles" (*O*, 248). Paz's change is from poetic values proclaiming a revolutionary position outside any system to one embodied in democracy. At least Paz's position is clear, and it does continue to place emphasis on action: "Freedom cannot be defined: it must be exercised" (*O*, 13).

Paz's activity can be summarized around two topics; Russian socialism and Sartre and Fourier. In 1951 Paz published a note with documentation concerning Stalin's concentration camps; since then Russia—its ideological rigidity, its terror, its crushing of dissidents—has epitomized the horrors of the twentieth century. Paz turns relentlessly against those who still follow Russia from poets like Neruda (*O*, 263) to Mexico's dogmatic left, and those who still think Russia offers a solution (Cuba, Nicaragua). Solzhenitsyn's case confirmed Paz's resistance to all state authoritarianism and became a test case of the writer's moral stance toward power. Paz confessed a moral sympathy for Solzhenitsyn (*O*, 247) and claimed that Solzhenitsyn had passed the test of history. One of the reasons Paz deduces for the collapse of Marxist-Leninism into terror was that power had become a caste, suppressing democracy. Paz blames Russia's ancient past, just as he had accused Mexico of its Aztec past. For Paz the *mito bolchevique* that he had once shared had degraded into a *peste autoritaria*. Two notions structure Paz's position: history as a testing ground of a writer's moral worth and democracy as a symbol of the writer's plurality or dialogue with self, reality, and others. [27]

Sartre becomes the other exemplary case (*O*, 308); his attack on Camus, his refusal to accept the evidence of the camps in Russia, his attack on Breton as well as his self-criticisms and mistakes have often been commented on by Paz over thirty years. Sartre stands for the disease of politics of this age; the wordy, opinionated intellectual, seduced by ideas, a Marxism that never really sustained a dialogue with history (*O*, 311). Paz brings out Sartre's moral blindness to specific differences where ideas (*sombras*/shadows) are more real than *dicha* (happiness) or *plenitud* (plenitude). Because of his influence in Latin America, Sartre became the negative side of being an intellectual in politics.

Against the empty promises of Marxism, Paz turned to democracy and Fourier rather than to poetry, as he did in the 1950s and 1960s. In 1972 Paz introduced Fourier to Mexico with an essay and Tomás Segovia's translation of Breton's long *Ode à Charles Fourier*. [28] And it is through Fourier that Paz still holds on to his Bretonian lineage; Fourier, the political antidote to the rotten twentieth century, for Fourier teaches man to believe in his body and instincts. For him the roots of social behavior are "atracción apasionada" (passionate attraction, *O*, 208). In his society work could be attractive; his protoecological stance rooted in an anti-industrial, anticonsumerist, and prodemographic control showed where socialism could have turned: into erotic freedom, cooperation, and sexual equality. For Paz Fourier will become more important than Marx; he is the "piedra de toque del siglo xx" (the touch stone of the twentieth century, O, 221).

India in Retrospect: Renga and el mono gramático

In 1968 Paz published what he called "Topoemas" in a magazine[29] then collected them in La centena (Hundred, an anthology, 1970) and finally in his Poemas. In a note he described these experimental texts as spacial poems in keeping with haiku, Apollinaire's calligrammes, and Brazilian concrete poetry. He dedicated them to friends like Cortázar and Fuentes. These pleasing visual puns play with words as signs, using capital letters, Paz's own handwriting, and shapes to exploit the word's potentials to contain other hidden meanings inside. One exposes a central tenet of Buddhism in a poem that looks calligraphic by playing with "Niego" (I negate) and "Ni-ego" (Not-ego) and Buddhism's argument by negation and denial of the reality of the ego (P, 501).[30] These word games were in the air, and Paz did not prolong this kind of experimentation.

A more far-reaching experiment centered round the collaborative writing of Renga in April 1969 in Paris. Four poets—Charles Tomlinson, Paz, Jacques Roubaud, and Eduardo Sanguinetti—wrote a chain of poems together, each one in his mother tongue, with translations on the other side of the page into one language. The revised rules of this Western renga led to using sonnets, chance associations, and four languages. The experiment was dedicated to André Breton, who invented several games (like le cadavre exquis) to break down the differences between poets and allow chance, shock and surprise to enter a text. With Paz there is the added metaphor: the brotherhood or community of modern poets (cf. Lautréamont's future society where all will be poets) as a myth of understanding beyond the limits of particular languages. What is interesting in all the poets (perhaps excluding Sanguinetti) is that they all know other languages and cultures and that the strangeness of the experiment becomes the main poetic topic. There is a genuine overlap of concerns (Provençal and Japanese poetry, Dante, Rimbaud, and Pound), and the artificial sonnet form is brought alive by the interplay of languages.

The event was clearly exciting, close to that getting-to-know-a-poet that is collaborative translation, what Roubaud in his note on the Japanese origins of *renga* calls a "spiritual exercise to penetrate the talent and vision of another."[31] The experience also confirmed Paz's belief that modern poetry is one tradition. But is it more than a fun game? The peculiar demands tend to bring out parodies of the best work of each poet when writing on his own. There is also a sense of virtuosity rather than humility and glib one-liners. The worst aspect is the coy self-awareness. The amusing part for the reader is identifying the voices and seeing if a collective voice does emerge. Certainly the idea of a *renga* as a meeting place of practicing poets—with the notions of criticizing solitary inspiration and humiliating the ego—made this a historic event that promised a future. Paz himself has continued to collaborate with Charles Tomlinson, writing poems around the themes of House and Day but in letters, published as *Airborn/Hijos del aire* (1981). *Renga* was first published in French (1971), then Spanish (1972), and finally English (1972), but Paz did not collect it in *Poemas*.

In 1974 Paz published one of his masterpieces, *El mono gramático*, written in 1970 and like *Renga* first published in French, still the most exciting edition to look at. But apart from coining the title, *Le singe grammairien,* himself, the French edition is a translation. This should not obscure the fact that Paz, like T. S. Eliot, Huidobro, César Moro, Juan Larrea, and others, did write poems in French, some collected in *Ladera este*.

The French title suggests a pun *singe/signe* (monkey/sign) and an opposition between monkey and grammar (in the West); the Spanish title keeps this opposition between human language that separates man from the natural world. In 1971 Paz published a fragment as "El simio gramático" suggesting further puns (simio/simil—simian/simile—proposed by Julián Ríos).[32] Language is at the core of this book. But the monkey association suggests that man is not severed from the natural world, for Hanumān, the flying, traveling monkey from the *Ramayana* (in the English epigraph) was also a grammarian. This Hanumān also links the other main topic: travel. The title of the first Skira edition's series was "Les sentiers de la création" (the paths of creation), which included texts by Henri Michaux, René Char, and Yves Bonnefoy. Paz merely elaborated on this creative path literally, linking a series of analogies: to write, to read, to walk, to travel, to trace, all metaphors of moving in time (life). On a realistic level Paz writes about a journey he and his wife made to

visit the ruins of Galta in India. Superimposed on this is the journey
his memory retraces; on this, the act of writing about this journey
where the writing is another journey in self-consciousness. This
same layering applies to a garden and some trees glimpsed from the
poet's writing table in Cambridge, England. The text confuses all
these layers, abolishing the literal, original journey. For the real
journey is the quest for self.

This analogy of walking along a path and writing or reading along
a line leads back to Hanumān who, in the *Ramayana,* contemplated
a garden as if it were a system of signs: the world as a book where
reading is decyphering correspondences. Paz invokes the magic word
como (like), as Breton had before,[33] for it promises the principle of
analogy: "en esto ver aquello" (in this see that, *P,* 581), Paz's motto
for alienated Western man to rejoin the cosmos.

El mono gramático is a poem written in prose. Paz once called it
a treatise (to Ríos), part novel, part reflection on language. The
confusion of genre is deliberate, echoing Paz's view that "poetry"
is what happens in your mind when you read where reading becomes
a process akin to the creative act. And process hints at temporality.
Formally this text may approach the prose poem, but within Paz's
aesthetics all static forms are converted into temporal structures
given life by the reader's erotic participation in its unfolding. Art
and life have no finality except death; the only purpose is to experience them as the now of a process in time.

Paz's prime analogy—path/sentence—suggests a pilgrimage; but
it is toward the elusive self rather than sacred Galta. Yet man is
only a perpetual possibility; there is no static solid self to find, only
a quest for self along a path of lineal words. Paz calls this "Búsqueda
del fin, terror ante el fin: el haz y el envés del mismo acto" (Quest
for the end, terror about the end: the front and back of the same
act, *P,* 509). The quest is never ending, it is life.

The poet, as he proceeds along the journey, conveys the rhythmic
ebb and flow of his mind and its memories: monkeys, ruins, stones,
a Holy man. Then these memories are blurred under the present
tense of a perception while writing about writing: a window, a tree,
a dustbin. Then another displacement and the poet stares at lovers's
shadows projected on to a wall. All these levels are interrelated in
the textual flow that itself becomes a metaphor for the mind set
free from its prison (of history, thought, and dead words). This
movement is further generated by sets of verbs: light up/go out,

appear/disappear, weave/unweave; the poet's path is not a straight line. Within the text there is a further mobility, partially lost in the Spanish version, instigated by the links and interplay between the stunning photographs of Galta, monkeys, Sadhus, and the dazzling reproductions of paintings by Brauner, Dadd, Balthus, Michaux, Toyen, and Paz's text, as if he wrote his text around these reproductions.

El mono gramático is also a treatise on language itself, continuing Mallarmé's "La destruction fut ma Béatrice" (Destruction was my Beatrice) cited in the text. The poet follows his thoughts as they coalesce into opaque words, then suddenly, after a patient wait, he sees on the page the "shadow of our thoughts, the reverse of what we see and talk and are" (P, 516). But he can see only during the actual moment of perception, thus deflating history by converting it into sensation. Paz's revenge: "wisdom is in what is instantaneous" (P, 513). During this epiphany opaque language is dissolved and the mind rid of its concepts and categories so that reality is seen as it is undeformed by wordiness, *sunyata*. Then the poet's dry brain is fertilized (Paz quoted T. S. Eliot from "Gerontion").

Everyday language cannot make sense of the ruins of Galta, of any ruins for "the universe is a senseless text" (P, 531). But if it lacks meaning, this universe can be grasped through the senses: "I can touch it but I cannot say it" (P, 533); only the senses can keep in touch with time's movement. In this text Paz has freed words from all fixity so that they flow and mirror time; Paz calls this act the abolition of differences, where the poet joins the monkey Hanumān and both rejoin the reality of the world beyond language, culture, and history.

Instead of naming and illusorily fixing, the poet dissolves words and reveals their emptiness, so that reality shines through: language made transparent. Reality seen directly through words is now a *desmesura* (excess). Sense is only granted in the now of the act of writing, the act of love: "All is now" (P, 573). The center is not at the end of the journey, for nothing happened at Galta. The point of *El mono gramático* is the actual pleasure of reading, making sense, being confused, and releasing one's potential for freedom through this multilayered experience. Paz names this experience *Esplendor*, an erotic woman's name, a quality of light, of life, the poet's wife and all women. She is *presencia* and the poet's reward is to fix his attention fully on this Other, now. Only face to face with "her" is there completion, is the journey worth while. Like *Blanco,* this poem is also a delightful philosophical love-song. And love silences history and recovers innocence as the poet learns from the Galta pilgrims: "But those who walked with me . . . had abolished distance— time, history, the line that separates man from the world. Their walking was a timeless ceremony of the abolition of differences. The pilgrims knew something I ignored: the noise of human syllables was one more rumor yet identical to the monkey screams, the parrot screams, and the lowing of the wind. Knowing this was to reconcile myself with time, to reconcile times" (*P,* 551).[34]

Pasado en claro

Paz's 1970–71 Eliot Norton lectures at Harvard, *Children of the Mire* (1974), continued to examine the tension between poet and society—for Paz, the secret theme of poetry since the romantic era—in modern poetry, the disguised religion of the modern age. Paz discusses analogy, religion, attitudes to revolutionary politics, tradition, and so on, without aspirations to writing literary history. In these lectures he turned to Wordsworth's stay in France and reaction against the French Revolution. Wordsworth resorted to childhood's "moments of translucency" to combat the disasters of history and revolutionary despotism. He became the first to see the tree, stone, and stream as they are. Paz labels Wordsworth's *The Prelude; or, Growth of a Poet's Mind* a vision of the other time different to history, dates, kings, gallows, and revolutions. Turning inward is the poet's revolutionary stance because he seeks the time before time, "la vie antérieure" (the title of a Baudelaire poem) which reappears in the child's glance.[35] Paz placed an epigraph from Wordsworth to his long poem on memory and childhood *Pasado en claro* (1975), adding notes in 1979.

Pasado en claro is part elegy for lost time, part autobiography, part defense of poetry from the "garrulous, ferocious" men in power. In its *vaivén* (oscillation) between the present act of writing and the nebulous personal past, this fine poem parallels *El mono gramático.*

As a moral act this poem retrieves the innocence of childhood not as a liberating romantic topos but as a moment when the poet simply ignored the corruptions of time and history. As a viable alternative to history this poem again articulates the inner space of memory seen as in "El balcón" as a balcony "inside me" (*P,* 613).[36]

Memory opens a window in the galleries of time to offer an image of *intocable realidad* (untouchable reality, *I*, 175). Paz situates his poem in a declining day and sunset that becomes a nocturnal meditation in a study in a city with a book of prints at hand, the poet guided by his faithful lamp (*P*, 650). The lyrical element of this poem arises both from the repeated "¿dónde estuve?" (where was I?) about his past and from rescuing images as words on paper from the ruins of time.

The poem begins as a monologue but veers away from private memory to affirm itself as a poem. Both *fresno* (ash) and *higuera* (fig-tree), key symbols to Paz's unique experiences, become converted by entering this poem to belong equally to the reader; from realities they end up as words.

Memory—mental thoughts, echoes—weaves the poet between his intangible past and his present where words are just "pauses" or "eddies" in the flow of time. Between his memories and the present lies a kind of doubt. From this elusive state of suspension the poet recalls, as words on paper, his childhood "ash" surrounded now by emptiness (the past is nowhere but an image in the emptiness of his mind). The poet as a child has become an image in his own eye. But he can re-create this lost "ash" with words so that it becomes a "sinuosa llama líquida" (a sinuous liquid flame, *P*, 644) and live again. Because of the transforming magic of language, the childhood garden is alive: the wall dense with life, fungae, lizards. The poet falls down the well into his past wonderland, his memories "un charco es mi memoria" (my memory a puddle, *P*, 646; a reference to the puddle with which Rimbaud ends his "Le Bateau ivre")[37]— all the richness of the past reduced to words. The poet recalls his boyish games, the solitary rituals round the fig tree:

> La hendedura fue pórtico
> del más allá de lo mirado y lo pensado:
> allá dentro son verdes las mareas,
> la sangre es verde, el fuego verde,
> entre las yerbas negras arden estrellas verdes:
> es la música verde de los élitros
> en la prístina noche de la higuera. . . .
>
> (*P*, 647)

(The fissure was gateway / to the beyond of what is seen and thought / there inside the tides are green, / blood is green, fire green, / among the black herbs green stars burn: / it is the green music of elytra / in the pristine night of the figtree.)

This fig-tree foretold another life, an alternative sensibility; the wisdom the fig-tree taught the young poet concerned the seasons and how to talk to himself.

The poet reviews his past spent reading adventure stories, poems, erotic novels as if he had undergone a druidic baptism—the tree, pillar, book, and mistletoe. But now his adolescence has vanished, as ephemeral as "clouds." The poet then conjures up the large family house in Mixcoac, the church, sugar cane—sensually re-created in a Carlos Pellicer–type image as "carabinas de azúcar" (rifles of sugar, P, 652)—and the colorful markets. But the house lies empty, family life over. Typical of this poem's ebb and flow (mind's movement), it becomes an eddy in the flow of life that has allowed the poet to be with himself inside the poem. Paz, a lonely child among adults, with his ash tree, his mother, aunt, grandfather, and a distant father with whom he could only talk in dreams.

As the poet grew up he learned to become a double of himself: "Hablé conmigo" (I talked with myself, P, 654). He never wanted to be a boss, gain a lucrative profession, or become a saint. Early on he discovered that his reality was *cuerpo* (the sign body), as his poem gives body to pale memories. But the crucial insight then was facing his own mortality. The word "death":

> El sonido, bastón de ciego del sentido:
> escribo *muerte* y vivo en ella
> por un instante. Habito su sonido:
> en un cubo neumático de vidrio,
> vibra sobre esta página,
> desaparece entre sus ecos.
>
> (P, 655)

(The sound, blindman's cane of sense: / I write *death* and live in it / for an instant. I inhabit its sound: / in a pneumatic cube of glass / it vibrates on this page, / disappears among its echoes.)

All that remains of his personal life is words and images in his mind written on this page. But there are "messengers." Man if he "listens" (this act of listening is central to the poem) can hear the universe talking through him:

Animales y cosas se hacen lenguas,
a través de nosotros habla consigo mismo
el universo. Somos un fragmento
—pero cabal en su inacabamiento—
de su discurso. . . .

                                    (*P*, 656)

(Animals and things become tongues, / through us the universe talks / to
itself. We are a fragment / —but consumate in its unfinishedness— / of
its discourse. . . .)

The universe talks in analogies and images, but does not possess a
meaning. Man's incompleteness (made relative by time and history)
is his truth. Paz's lovely aphorism recalls Yves Bonnefoy's "L'imperfection est la cime" (Imperfection is the peak).[38] For Paz the
discovery of death initiated him into time and history; his realization
that all was doomed, even his childhood games: "ser tiempo es la
condena, nuestra pena es la historia" (to be time is the condemnation,
our penalty is history, *P*, 657). Confrontation with this insight tests
a man's worth. It is curious that by 1974 Paz's opposition to history
is not so radically certain; note his perhaps: "El escape, quizás, es
hacia dentro" (escape, perhaps, is inside ourselves, *P*, 657). But the
poet's escape from history is to purge language, dissolve the pronouns (as in *El mono gramático*) to find his "más ser sin yo" (more
being without the ego, *P*, 657) and recover anonymous being.
    The poet shares the Mallarmean "néant," the "plenitud vacía"
(empty plenitude), as the only exorcism of the noise of history and
its corrupt idioms. This *nada* (the nothing that makes up being)
has accompanied him since his early dialogues with the fig-tree,
but he could never name it: "Fatigué el cubilete y el *ars combinatoria*"
(I tired the dice box and the combinatory art, *P*, 659—cf. Mallarmé's *Un coup de dés*). Against power and history Paz creates this
poem:

Espiral de los ecos, el poema
es aire que se esculpe y se disipa,
fugaz alegoría de los nombres
verdaderos. . . .

                                    (*P*, 660)

(Spiral of echoes, the poem / is air that sculpts itself and dissipates itself /
fleeting allegory of the true / names. . . .)

The poem is air (wind, breathing) that resists history because it is
fleeting (faithful to time) and because it is a mental act. But the
poem does hint at the truth that words can never trap, at a reconciliation with the universe and life. Suddenly on a page the signs
of sounds and sense burst into "magnetic" life (magnetic, Breton's
favorite word). The poet's identity is created by this poem, by the
"murmurs" (sounds of words) the poet hears as he thinks. These
words have more life than his memories, than his past life. The
poem ends: "Soy la sombra que arrojan mis palabras" (I am the
shadow that my words cast, *P, 660*); the poet dispensable, a shadow,
compared to the life of these words in his poem transformed by a
reader. The poet's identity solidifies in the process of making the
poem (cf. the previously quoted Mallarméan process: in front of the
paper the poet makes himself). Like Wordsworth's *Prelude*, Paz's
Pasado en claro outlines the growth and making of a universal poet
from Mexico.[39]

Vuelta

In 1976 Paz collected his poems from 1968 to 1975 in *Vuelta*
the title of a poem and of his magazine. At a formal level these
poems prolong the spacialization of words begun in *Salamandra* and
carry notes at the end. There are fewer love poems and more circumstantial ones: memory and the degraded state of Mexico are the
main themes. And there is still the T. S. Eliot search for "water":
"¿Dónde está el agua otra?" (where is the other water, *P, 612*), the
last line of "Petrificada petrificante" (Petrified petrifying) that repeats his "¿Dónde está el otro mar? (where is the other sea, *P, 333*)
of *Salamandra* (1962). In this book's neologisms and wordplay Paz
recalls Huidobro's *Altazor* (1931), whose later cantos he much
admires.

Most of the poems are dedicated to friends. "Arboleda" (Grove),
dedicated to Pere Gimferrer and dated Cambridge, 1971, refers to
the same trees, patio, and dustbin that appear in *El mono gramático*.
The poet turns this grove into words and creates the analogy between
falling night blurring out the distinctive details and words hardening
on a page, making rigid the movements of life. He resolves the
poem in the last line: "Poco a poco se petrifican los nombres" (little
by little the names petrify, *P, 590*). The trees are only brought to
life in the grove of words in the poet's mind. Once externalized on

to paper, these words—without the poet's or reader's re-creation of them—petrify.

Vuelta differs from previous collections because history intrudes into the poems, overlapping Paz's political oppositions of the 1970s in Mexico (dialogue, democracy). Rather than affirming and illustrating the poem as inner space/freedom, the poem itself is converted into the battle ground. "Vuelta" (written June 1971) exemplifies this new direction.

This poem describes Paz's return to Mexico (cf. his letter-epilogue to Ríos's *Solo a dos voces*), now an "edén subvertido" (subverted Eden; from his López Velarde epigraph about the destruction of the Catholic provinces during the Mexican Revolution) and his shock at seeing Mexico degraded by modern progress, capitalist lucre, megalomaniac government, and the sordid fantasies of the middle class. And the Aztec past still lives. The poem is dense with allusions: López Velarde, Shiki, Wang Wei, Tablada, Mallarmé, some of Paz's early poems, the nahuatl word "burning water," and so on.[40] It opens with the noise of the city and the poet returning to the home of his infancy in Mixcoac. He finds an image for 1970s Mexico: "En los buzones / se pudren las cartas" (in the letter boxes / letters rot, *P, 597*), implying absence of communication and hopeless bureaucracy. Then he slips back in memory, a "balcón / sobre el vacío" (balcony over emptiness, *P, 598*), an image often used. Tortured by the omnivorous presence of the alienating city, his past is *bruma* (mist) and his present a version of hell. Paz's packed sentences and sounds mimic nightmare city life that permeates everything from sex to cinemas and words. Power crazed "vultures" and "coyotes" reign over everything. The consonantal sounds of his lines convey his disgust: "Ciudad / montón de palabras rotas" (city/heap of broken words, *P, 600*) echo his earlier "El cántaro roto." Mexico City's only value is being branded with the dollar sign. The poet than asks himself what he has achieved in his life against the city: "¿Gané o perdí?" (did I win or lose?, *P, 601*). Unlike Wang Wei, he does not wish to escape these times. More urgently, he affirms: "El espacio está adentro" (space is inside, *P, 601*), the heartbeat of pure time. The wind blows the poplars as the poet continues to be buffeted by time: "Camino sin avanzar / Nunca llegamos" (I walk without advancing / we never arrive, *P, 602*). As in *Pasado en claro*, the poet is less optimistic about antidotes to history while affirming that surviving alive is all that counts.

This sense of uncertainty in the middle of life's journey is de-
veloped in "A la mitad de esta frase" (In the middle of this sentence),
again in terms of Mexico City with the poet in search of illumination,
stuck in a lift in the nightmarish city. All he can salvage from his
life, which is not a sea cruise, is the act of writing: "Estoy / en la
mitad de esta frase. / ¿Hacia dónde me lleva?" (I am / in the middle
of this sentence. / Where will it lead me?, P, 603). He recalls
Huidobro in his answer: "mi nacicaída" (my bornfall, P, 603).[41]
The finality of living puzzles the poet: he can only affirm that he
is where he is—writing, in the middle of a sentence and standing
in the ruins of his family home (as a new block is being built), in
a "pause" of time, an "ir y venir sin fin, sin comienzo" (a coming
and going without end, without beginning, P, 605). The poem
ends with the poet defining himself: "Poeta: jardinero de epitafios"
(poet: gardener of epitaphs, P, 606), in the rubbish dump of history.

    "Nocturno de San Ildefonso" (Nocturne of San Ildefonso) justifies
the whole collection. The poet, looking out of his window at night,
catches the signs and seeds that "night" suggests to his mind. The
window is also a tunnel: "Estoy a la entrada de un túnel" (I am at
the entrance of a tunnel, P, 630); only words can guide him in his
disorientation. As he speaks—"hablo con los ojos cerrados" (I speak
with my eyes closed, P, 630)—somebody, a force beyond his will
and control, changes his words magnetically. He leaps back to 1931
(the year he published his first poem), his personal history now
"broken images" (P, 632). He recalls his comrades as the night life
of the city enters the poem and interferes with the lineal flow of
memory. The adolescent of seventeen and the poet of sixty meet in
the poem. Paz's past has become a *mea culpa* of a generation who
for a while were seduced by Stalin and Revolution:

    El bien, quisimos el bien:
                    enderezar al mundo.
    No nos faltó entereza:
                    nos faltó humildad.
    Lo que quisimos no lo quisimos con inocencia.
    Preceptos y conceptos,
                    soberbia de teólogos. . . .
                                        (P, 634)

(Good, we wanted good / to right the world. / We did not lack integrity: /
we lacked humility. / What we wanted we did not want with innocence /
Precepts and concepts / pride of theologians.)

The poet curses this "comunión obligatoria" (obligatory commun-ion, *P*, 634), and some of his friends have continued to toe the party line by becoming secretaries to the Party, with hate as a philosophy, their arid reasoning leading to the *patíbulo* (gallows, *P*, 634) and adoration by the millions. Paz has re-created his guilty antipathy to doctrinaire Marxism; his own involvement, retractions, silences, and changes. But his history was not an error, history itself is. Human truth lay beyond dates and names; it is the "anonymous heartbeat of life" (*P*, 635). This is no longer an epiphanic view but simply consciousness of being alive: "Oculto, inmóvil, intocable, / el presente—no sus presencias—está siempre" (hidden, immobile, untouchable / the present, not its presences, is always, *P*, 636). This defense of the heartbeat of the present, a humble alternative to history, finds its political analogy in Paz's defense of democratic values (not a Blakean or a surrealist revolution) against authority, power, and money.

But it is as a poet—"dar ojos al lenguaje" (to give eyes to lan-guage, *P*, 636)—resurrecting the full living richness of words that Paz has fulfilled his destiny, his duty. Poetry points to this "verdad del tiempo no fechado" (truth of undated time, *P*, 636), the intense present of experience that all men and women share. Paz defines this almost politically in a lovely expression:

> La verdad:
> sabemos,
> desde el origen,
> suspendidos.
> Fraternidad sobre el vacío.
>
> (*P*, 637)

(The truth / we know / from the origins / suspended. / Fraternity above emptiness.)

Paz has found another sense to fraternity from the socialist one of the 1930s: it is all humankind. All that is left of Paz's life in history is language; words in a poem. His poem ends with the poet glancing at the mystery of his sleeping wife, her flowing, sensual inner visions, his other. As dawn breaks (similarly in many of Paz's in-somniac night thoughts), the poet affirms his blood circulating in his head, the joy of being alive next to his wife "fuente en la noche" (fountain in the night, *P, 639*). The last line is optimistic: "Yo me fío a su fluir sosegado" (I trust myself to her calm flow, *P, 639*) where she is both wife and muse, woman and word, love and language. That is the poet's act of faith in his disturbing times.

Paz's dedication to woman has obeyed a personal vocation within a greater historical context that includes his repudiation of Mexican *machismo* and his support for Breton's surrealism and its literary tradition in favor of woman as man's only radical Other. The woman who figures constantly in his poems oscillates between a real historical woman and an idea, an archetype, a muse, an anima, a myth, both initiatrix and mediatrix.[42] To some this single-minded dedication to woman may seem out of tune with aspects of feminism as too exclusive, even sexist an angle. Xavière Gauthier in *Surréalisme et sexualité* (1968) criticized the surrealists for sacralizing and derealizing woman and converting her into an ideal partner, the missing half, on a pedestal, a life/death, movement/repose universal principle.[43] In a sense Paz belongs to this Bretonian tradition, yet Gauthier condoned Paz's female as she appears in his prose poem "Mariposa de obsidiana" as more real than man's facile compliment, the weak negative of the male poet.[44]

The closest sources to Paz's fusion of a real with a symbolic woman in his concept of self-transcendence through this Other derive from André Breton (and lead back to Novalis) and Antonio Machado. In Breton's *Arcane 17* (1947) we read that woman is a pure being in communication with the elemental forces of nature, despite her present-day role in society. Woman is a form of presence who can redeem man from alienation. She becomes "earthly health."[45] Antonio Machado's idea about the heterogeneity of being (used as the epilogue to *El laberinto de la soledad*) was equally decisive as an influence, as Paz confessed to Julián Ríos. Paz admitted preferring Machado's apocryphal erotic philosopher Abel Martín whose views on love and woman clarify Paz's ambiguous woman. For Abel Martín love becomes the means to self-revelation. The loved one is absent and desired in the poet's mind. She is the "metaphysical thirst for what is essentially other."[46]

By the time that woman emerges as a sign on a page it is this mental otherness that Paz invokes, an otherness encouraged by the fact that Paz often camouflages the identity of his actual companion by associating her with all women, as he had done in *Piedra de sol* where she combines Mélusine, Laura, Isabel, Persephone, and María.

That Paz's dedication to the female muse is provocative and traditional (close to Robert Graves's white goddess) is underlined by the act of faith implicit in the verb that ends "Nocturno de San Ildefonso" where Paz emphasizes the "I": "Yo me fío . . ." (*P*, 639).

Conclusion

In 1979 Paz published his complete poems, though loyal to his notion of the lack of completion and finality in life, modestly calling it *Poemas (1935–1975)*. In a way, this compilation is a new version of his life work for Paz has updated, eliminated, corrected, and added notes and reminiscenses. His poetics of the "now" oblige him to review his work, from the now of 1979. But in a curious way this is purifying from history exactly that which makes history such a pervasive enemy. My study has attempted in a general narrative way to situate Paz's work within the often silent contexts of history. A rereading of Paz awaits another critic from the perspective of Paz's revisionist *Poemas*.

In 1982 Paz published his long detailed study of Sor Juana Inés de la Cruz (1648–95) called *Sor Juana Inés de la Cruz o las trampas de la fe*, (Sor Juana Inés de la Cruz or the traps of faith) literally a lifetime's devotion to this underrated baroque poet. Paz wrote his first essay on Sor Juana in 1950 (published in *Pe*, 38–54). This magnificent book combines strict historical scholarship with wideranging speculations and asides from anthropological insights to modern poetry, totalitarian states, and courtly love with autobiographical allusions. Particularly interesting is the relationship between Paz writing in the twentieth century and Sor Juana's struggle to be a scholar and a poet in the repressive society of New Spain. This book deepens historically Paz's investigation into freedom by enmeshing Sor Juana in her times, in its hierarchies, rituals, and codes; a woman in a man's world, eventually silenced. Her enigma fascinates Paz, and this is a study of difference and otherness (a woman; New Spain; the church) based on secret affinities (being a learned poet; totalitarianism).

The starting point and the book's secondary title, "the traps of faith," emerges in Paz's view of the poet. What he calls the terrible readers, in Sor Juana's times the archbishop, the Inquisition, and in his own the secretary general of the Party, the Politbureau,[47] determine the poet's work. All his study explores *"what cannot be said"* (*So,* 117). To reverse this premise and apply it to Paz himself, along far more general lines, has been the aim of this book: Paz has written an ethical poetry in a dogmatically politicized and materialistic age that despises the values of poetry.

If we review all Paz's work and ask which book best unites his mind and sensibility we would have selected *El mono gramático,* followed by *Pasado en claro* and *Piedra de sol.* But also important is *Sor Juana Inés de la Cruz,* a "poem" in the sense that Paz defines it, surrealistically: a text that sparks off poetry, an inner adventure, in a reader. Paz's latest book meanders between biography, history, literary criticism, intellectual speculation, and numerous asides to become itself a metaphor of freedom, embodying what he once wrote about Lévi-Strauss's style—which "oscillates continually between the concrete and the abstract, the direct intuition of the object and analysis: a mind that sees ideas as sensuous forms and forms as intellectual signs" (*Cl,* 11).

Since *Vuelta* (1976), his last collection of poems, Paz has continued to publish poems and has collected his notes, comments, and reviews. It would be foolish to predict a new style, though the poems that stretch from *Salamandra* (1962) to *Vuelta* seem to have rounded off into a cycle. Can we expect a change as radical as the later W. B. Yeats's? Some poems like "Ejercicio preparatorio" (Preparation exercise)[48] or "Raíces ramas sílabas" (Roots branches syllables)[49] tentatively point to a new concision, less dependent on cultural associations and dealing more directly with the *condena* (condemnation) of time. But whatever Paz's new departures, the constant that this study has attempted to expose, Paz's temporal poetics offering momentary breaks but no privileged escapes from history and time still stands. For Paz in a socially urgent and responsible way has made poetry an ethical guide that creates spaces for inner values, the adventures and thrills of consciousness that refuses to categorize life along given lines and thus negate love, imagination, fantasy, and art. All his life as a writer Paz has fought explicitly at the level of topics and themes and implicitly at the level of values for art to "help man resist and persist" (*Pu,* 108). And this art must change life, a collective alternative act to revolutionary politics. In 1966 he diagnosed: "The West must rediscover the secret of the incarnation of the poem into collective life, the fiesta" (*C,* 217).

Notes and References

Chapter One

1. See Rita Guibert, *Seven Voices* (New York: Vintage Books, 1973); Alfredo Roggiano, "Persona y ámbito de Octavio Paz," in *Octavio Paz* (Madrid, 1979), 5–33.
2. See Henry C. Schmidt, *The Roots of Lo Mexicano: Self and Society in Mexican Thought 1900–1934* (College Station: Texas A. & M. Press, 1978), Martin Stabb, *In Quest of Identity: Patterns in the Spanish American Essay of Ideas, 1890–1960* (Chapel Hill: University of North Carolina Press, 1967), and A. P. Debicki, *Antología de la poesía mexicana moderna* (London: Tamesis Books Ltd., 1976).
3. "Constante amigo," *Taller* 4 (July 1939):53.
4. *El arco y la lira* (Mexico City, 1967), 172; hereafter cited in the text as *A*.
5. *Las peras del olmo* (Mexico City, 1965), 76; hereafter cited in the text as *Pe*.
6. *El ogro filantrópico: Historia y política 1971–78* (Mexico City, 1979), 20; hereafter cited in the text as *O*.
7. *El laberinto de la soledad* (Mexico, 1964), 24; hereafter cited in the text as *L*.
8. *Hombres en su siglo y otros ensayos* (Barcelona, 1984), 37; hereafter cited in the text as *H*.
9. See Jason Wilson, *Octavio Paz: A Study of his Poetics* (Cambridge, 1979), 30.
10. "Respuesta y algo más," *México en la cultura* 569 (February 1960):7.
11. Hugo Verani, "Octavio Paz y el primer poema," *Revista de la universidad de México* 12 (April 1982):3.
12. See M. Forster, *An Index to Mexican Literary Periodicals* (New York: Scarecrow Press, 1966).
13. Dolores de la Mora, "¿Cómo nace un poeta?" *El Gallo ilustrado* 68 (13 October 1963):1; Luis Mario Schneider, "Historia singular de un poema de Octavio Paz," in *Aproximaciones a Octavio Paz*, ed. Angel Flores, (Mexico City, 1974), 113–17.
14. *Prosas profanas* (Madrid: Espasa-Calpe, 1964), 13.
15. X. Villaurrutia, *Obras* (Mexico City: F.C.E., 1966), 46–47. See Wilson, *Octavio Paz*, 10–13 and Paz, *Xavier Villaurrutia en persona y en obra* (Mexico City, 1978); hereafter cited in the text as *X*.
16. Guibert, *Seven Voices*, 232.

144 OCTAVIO PAZ

17. See M. Forster, *Los Contemporáneos 1920–1932: Perfil de un experimento vanguardista* (Mexico City: Ediciones de Andrea, 1964).
18. Julián Ríos, *Solo a dos voces* (Barcelona: Editorial Lumen, 1973), unpaged.
19. Villaurrutia, *Obras*, 641–59, 773–83. See Allen Phillips "Octavio Paz: Critic of Modern Mexican Poetry," in *The Perpetual Present: The Poetry and Prose of Octavio Paz*, ed. I. Ivask, (Norman, 1973), 61.
20. "El testimonio de los sentidos," *Romance* 3 (March 1940):9.
21. "Razón de ser," *Taller* 2 (April 1932):32.
22. *Sombras de obras: Arte y literatura* (Barcelona, 1983), p. 104; hereafter cited in the text as *S*.
23. Villaurrutia, *Obras*, 772.
24. *Poesía en movimiento: México 1915–1966* (Mexico City: Siglo XXI, 1966), 16; hereafter cited in the text as *Po*.
25. *Libertad bajo palabra: Obra poética (1935–1957)* (Mexico City, 1968), 87; hereafter cited in the text as *Li*.
26. See R. Phillips, *The Poetic Modes of Octavio Paz* (Oxford, 1972), 8–10; C. Magis, *La poesía hermética de Octavio Paz* (Mexico City, 1978), 19–23.
27. Ríos, *Solo a dos voces*.
28. "Rafael Alberti, visto y entrevisto," *El país*, 4 June 1984, 9.
29. *El nacional*, 4 October 1936, 7.
30. Cited by K. Muller-Bergh, "La poesía de Octavio Paz en los años treinta," in *Octavio Paz*, ed. A. Roggiano, 67.
31. Hugh Thomas, *The Spanish Civil War* (Harmondsworth: Penguin Books, 1965), 631; Valentine Cunningham, ed., *Spanish Civil War Verse* (Harmondsworth: Penguin Books, 1980), 47; Juan Gil-Albert, *Memorabilia* (Barcelona: Tusquets Editor, 1975), 229–32, 252.
32. Guibert, *Seven Voices*, 212.
33. Ibid., 213.
34. C. Couffon, "Entrevista con Octavio Paz," *Cuadernos* 36 (May–June 1959):80.
35. S. Spender, *World within World* (London: Hamish Hamilton, 1951), 242.
36. C. Connolly, "The Pen and the Sword," *Sunday Times*, 13 April 1969, 3.
37. Elena Poniatowski, "Octavio Paz: Roca solar de la poesía," *México en la cultura* 450 (3 November 1957):3.
38. Cunningham, *Spanish Civil War Verse*, 59.
39. Published in *Hora de España* 9 (September 1937):39, 41.
40. "Oda al sueño," first published in *Taller* 4 (July 1939):36–39.
41. "Oda a España," first published in *Letras de México* 30 (1 August 1938):3.

42. "Oda al sueña," 36.
43. Ibid., 38.
44. Ibid., 39.
45. Noted by Muller-Bergh, "La poesía de Octavio Paz," 69.
46. Published in *Poesía* 3 (May 1938):16.
47. Published as a supplement to *Tierra nueva* 9–10 (January–April 1942), unpaged.
48. See Judith Goetzinger, "Evolución de un poema: Tres versiones de *Bajo tu clara sombra*," in *Octavio Paz*, ed. A. Roggiano, 73–106.
49. Couffon, "Entrevista," 80.
50. Juan Gil-Albert, "Octavio Paz," *Hora de España* 11 (November 1937):76.
51. R. Solanas, *Las revistas literarias de México* (Mexico: I.N.B.A., 1963), 98; E. Abreu Gómez in *Ruta* 8 (January 1939):54.
52. In *Taller* 3 (May 1939):42.
53. Ibid., 42–43.
54. Published in *Taller* 10 (March–April 1940):29.
55. Laus, "Octavio Paz hoy: la crítica de la significación," *Diorama de la cultura*, 16 April 1967, 1.
56. *Voces de España: Breve antología de poetas españoles contemporáneos* (Mexico City: Ediciones Letras de México, 1938); letter in *Letras de México* 31 (15 September 1938):11.
57. In *Taller* 7 (December 1939):19.
58. *Puertas al campo* (Mexico City, 1966), 212; hereafter cited in the text as *Pu*.
59. *Taller* 7 (December 1939):19.
60. Cited in H. Verani, *Octavio Paz: Bibliografía crítica* (Mexico City: U.N.A.M., 1983).
61. *Tierra nueva* 7–8 (January–April 1941):34.
62. R. Xirau, *Tres poetas de la soledad* (Mexico City: Antigua Librería Robredo, 1955) and *Octavio Paz: El sentido de la palabra* (Mexico City, 1970).
63. *Tierra nueva* 7–8 (January–April 1941):34.
64. Ibid., 37–38.
65. Ibid., 39–40.
66. "Avec tes yeux je change comme avec les lunes / Et je suis tour à tour et de plomb et de plume, / Une eau mystérieuse et noire qui t'enserre . . ." (Eluard, *Capitale de la douleur* [Paris: Gallimard, 1966], 79). Paz translated Eluard in *Versiones y diversiones* (Mexico City: Joaquín Mortiz, 1974).
67. Pablo Neruda, *Confieso que he vivido: Memorias* (Buenos Aires: Editorial Losada, 1974), 177–78.
68. "Pablo Neruda en el corazón," *Ruta* 4 (15 September 1938):25.

69. Ibid., 25.
70. Ibid., 31.
71. Ibid., 33.
72. Neruda, *Confieso*, 223.
73. *Letras de México* 8 (15 August 1943):5. For a commentary on this feud see E. Rodríguez Monegal, *El viajero inmóvil: Introducción a Pablo Neruda* (Buenos Aires: Editorial Losada, 1966), 106.
74. Couffon, "Entrevista," 80.
75. "Apuntes sobre 'La realidad y el deseo,' " in *Corriente alterna*. (Mexico City, 1967), 15; hereafter cited as *C* in the text. Paz has returned to his friendship with Cernuda in "Juegos de memoria y olvido," *Vuelta* 108 (November 1985):27–32.
76. Abreu Gómez, *"Entre la piedra y la flor,"* *Tierra nueva* 9–10 (May–August 1941):174.
77. R. Salazar Mallén, *Las ostras o la literatura* (Mexico City: Porrúa y Obregón, 1958), 49.
78. Raúl Leiva, "Un nuevo libro de Octavio Paz: *Semillas para un himno,*" *México en la cultura* 298 (5 December 1954):2.
79. E. Carballo, *Diecinueve protagonistas de la literatura mexicana del siglo XX* (Mexico City: Empresas Editoriales, 1965), 446.

Chapter Two

1. See Forster, *An Index,* for details. Paz commented on these translations in "El surrealismo es uno," an interview with E. Rodríguez Monegal and R. González Echevarría, *Convergencias/divergencias/incidencias* (Barcelona: Tusquets Editor, 1973), 176–79.
2. In *Taller* 2, no. 10 (March–April 1940). The poems translated include "The Love Song of J. Alfred Prufrock," "La Figlia Che Piange," "The Hollow Men," "Ash Wednesday," and "The Waste Land." On Paz and T. S. Eliot see Judith M. Hoover, "The Urban Nightmare: Alienation Imagery in the Poetry of T. S. Eliot and Octavio Paz," *Journal of Spanish Studies* 1 (Spring 1978):13–28.
3. Luis Cernuda, *La realidad y el deseo (1924–1962)* (Mexico City: Fondo de Cultura Económica, 1964), 69.
4. Ibid., 68.
5. A. Camus, *L'Homme révolté,* in *Oeuvres complètes* (Paris: Imprimerie Nationale, 1962), 3:229.
6. In P. Waldberg, *Surrealism* (London: Thames & Hudson, 1965), 24.
7. R. Caillois, *Cases d'un échiquier* (Paris: Gallimard, 1970), 210–12.
8. On Breton in Mexico see Wilson, *Octavio Paz,* 15–16, and

L. M. Schneider, *México y el surrealismo (1925–1950)* (Mexico City: Arte y Libros, 1978), 109–66.

9. For the details see Wilson, *Octavio Paz,* 20–33. For the Parisian background consult J. L. Bédouin, *Vingt ans de surréalisme, 1939–1959* (Paris: Denoel, 1961); Alain Jouffroy, *Le Roman vécu* (Paris: Robert Laffont, 1978). On the magazines and art see Dawn Ades, *Dada and Surrealism Reviewed* (London: Arts Council of Great Britain, 1978).

10. See Wilson, *Octavio Paz,* 22–26; Lloyd King, "Surrealism and the Sacred in the Aesthetic Credo of Octavio Paz," *Hispanic Review* 37 (July 1969):382–93, and D. Martínez Torrón, *Variables poéticas de Octavio Paz* (Madrid, 1979), 54–69, for other views.

11. Couffon, "Entrevista," 80.

12. For Péret in Mexico see Schneider, *México,* 187–94.

13. See Wilson, *Octavio Paz,* 31.

14. Couffon, "Entrevista," 80.

15. "Benjamin Péret," *Les Lettres Nouvelles* 7, no. 24 (October 1959):27.

16. B. Péret, *Le Deshonneur des poètes* (Paris: Pauvert, 1965): "Le poète lutte contre toute oppression de sa pensée par les dogmes religieux, philosophiques ou sociaux" (75).

17. Paz, "Benjamin Péret," 27.

18. C. Monsiváis, "Octavio Paz en diálogo," *Revista de la universidad de México* 22, no. 3 (November 1967):8.

19. Paz, *In/mediaciones* (Barcelona, 1979), 148, 150; hereafter cited in the text as *I.*

20. Breton, *Clair de terre* (Paris: Gallimard, 1966), 157.

21. For an analysis of "El prisionero" see Wilson, *Octavio Paz,* 34–43.

22. See ibid., 31.

23. Jorge Guillén, *Obra poética* (Madrid: Alianza Editor, 1970), 35–39, 59–60. See Paz's analysis of Guillén's "Más allá," in *I,* 71–96. Paz also wrote on Guillén in *Pu,* 75–85.

24. Julio Cortázar, "Octavio Paz: *Libertad bajo palabra,*" in *Octavio Paz,* ed. A. Roggiano, 109.

25. "Tout porte à croire qu'il existe un certain point de l'esprit . . ." (in *Manifestes du surréalisme,* by A. Breton [Paris: Pauvert, 1962], p. 154; cited by Paz in *A,* 155, and *Pe,* 181).

26. César Vallejo, *Poesía completa* (Barcelona: Barral Editor, 1978), 432.

27. Ramón López Velarde, *Poesías completas* (Mexico City: Editorial Porrúa, 1968), 185.

28. Juan Gil-Albert, *Memorabilia,* 204.

29. Guibert, *Seven Voices,* 213.

30. E. Carballo, "Octavio Paz: su poesía convierte en poetas a sus lectores," *México en la cultura* 493 (25 August 1958):3.

31. For this background consult Stabb, *In Quest of Identity,* 197–209.

32. E. Carballo, "La respuesta de Emmanuel Carballo a Octavio Paz," *México en la cultura* 562 (21 December 1959):12.

33. "Respuesta y algo más" (1960), 2.

34. Ibid., 7.

35. See Sartre's attack on surrealism in his *Situations II: Qu'est-ce que la littérature?* (Paris: Gallimard, 1948). On the Sartre/Camus polemic look at J. Cruickshank *Albert Camus and the Literature of Revolt* (Oxford: Oxford University Press, 1960), 120–27.

36. James Joyce, *Ulysses* (London: Bodley Head, 1956), 34.

37. See Thomas Mermall, "Octavio Paz: *El laberinto de la soledad* y el sicoanálisis de la historia," *Cuadernos americanos* 367–68 (January–February 1968):97–114.

38. André Breton, *Le surréalisme et la peinture* (Paris: Gallimard, 1968), 230–34.

39. On the prose poem, see Wilson, *Octavio Paz,* 151–56.

40. André Breton told Rafael Valle in "Diálogo con Breton," *Universidad de Mexico* 29 (June 1938):6, that Mexico was a surrealist country. Paz's Mexico is "Un país que nunca ha podido vestir con entera corrección el traje de la civilización racionalista" (*Pe,* 57).

41. Charles Baudelaire, *Les fleurs du mal* (Paris: Editions de Cluny, 1841), 11.

42. Jorge Luis Borges: "No sé cual de los dos escribe esta página," in *Obras completas* (Buenos Aires: Emecé, 1974), 808. See E. Rodríguez Monegal, "Borges and Paz: Toward a Dialogue of Critical Texts," in *The Perpetual Present,* ed. I. Ivask, 45–52.

43. See "Dormir" or "Mon roi" from Henri Michaux, *La Nuit remue* or "Le honteux interne": "Voici déjà un certain temps que je m'observe sans rien dire, d'un oeil méfiant" or "Un homme perdu": "En sortant je m'égarai," in *La Nuit remue* (Paris: Gallimard, 1967), 115, 120. Paz translated Michaux in *Versiones y diversiones.*

44. Guibert, *Seven Voices,* 240.

45. In *Almanach surréaliste du demi-siècle,* special no. of *La Nef* 63–64 (March–April 1950):29–31. See Wilson, *Octavio Paz,* 25–27.

46. I. Nicholson, *Mexican and Central American Mythology* (London: Paul Hamlyn, 1967), 109.

47. Ibid., 112.

48. Arthur Rimbaud, *Oeuvres complètes* (Paris: Gallimard, 1972), 106.

49. On Paz's use of *stone* see D. Gallagher, *Modern Latin American Literature* (Oxford: Oxford University Press, 1973), 74; Elsa Dehennin,

"Stone and Water Imagery in Paz's Poetry," in *The Perpetual Present,* ed. I. Ivask 97–105; Magis, *La poesía,* 322–26.

50. Paz on poetry's "vocación revolucionaria" (*A,* 36); on poetry being "la más revolucionaria de las revoluciones" (*A,* 241).

51. André Breton: " 'Transformer le monde' a dit Marx; 'changer la vie' a dit Rimbaud: ces deux mots d'ordre pour nous n'en font qu'un" (*Manifestes,* 285).

52. Paz: "Los partidos políticos modernos convierten al poeta en propagandista y así lo degradan" (*A,* 41).

53. Paz quotes from B. Péret, *Le déshonneur . . .* (in *A,* 277–78).

54. E. Carballo, "Octavio Paz," 3.

55. T. S. Eliot, *Collected Poems 1909–1962* (London: Faber & Faber, 1963), 65.

56. Published in *Cuadernos americanos* 57 (May–June 1951):278–81.

57. See Paz on his own poem "Fuente" to E. Carballo, "Octavio Paz," 3.

58. Paz derived this stance from André Breton (see *Pe,* 171).

59. See Paz's prologue "Poesía en movimiento" in *Poesía en movimiento,* 3–34.

60. Paz in dialogue with E. Carballo, "Octavio Paz," 3. Read Paz on Mutra in *A,* 127–28.

61. Eliot, *Collected Poems,* 40.

62. Rimbaud, *Oeuvres,* 249–50.

63. As Paz said to E. Carballo, "Octavio Paz," 3.

Chapter Three

1. Eliot, *Collected Poems,* 63.

2. Ibid., 63–64, 90.

3. Paz: "Quizá, entonces, empezaremos a soñar otra vez con los ojos cerrados" (*L,* 176). See Jason Wilson, *"Abrir/cerrar los ojos:* a Recurrent Theme in the Poetry of Octavio Paz," *Bulletin of Hispanic Studies* 48, no. 1 (January 1971):44–56.

4. See Wilson, *Octavio Paz,* 18 for further details.

5. Ibid., 19, for further details.

6. Ibid.

7. In the words of Margarita Michelena, *Notas en torno a la poesía mexicana contemporánea* (Mexico City: Asociación Mexicana por la Libertad de la Cultura, 1956), 33.

8. See Wilson, *Octavio Paz,* 20, and José Emilio Pacheco, "Descripción de *Piedra de sol,"* in *Aproximaciones,* ed. Angel Flores, 182.

9. R. Leiva, *"Piedra de sol,"* *México en la cultura* 449 (27 October 1957):2.

10. A. Silva Villalobos, "Octavio Paz: *Semillas para un himno,*" *Metáfora* 3 (May–June 1955):37–38.

11. Pacheco, "Descripción," 182.

12. A. Lunel, "Octavio Paz: *Semillas para un himno,*" *México en la cultura* 311 (6 March 1955):2.

13. R. Xirau, "*Semillas para un himno,*" and Alí Chumacero, "Las letras mexicanas en 1954," *Universidad de México* 9, nos. 5–6 (January–February 1955):28, 8.

14. Compare Vicente Aleixandre's "La palabra": "La palabra fue un día / calor: un labio humano. / Era la luz como mañana joven; más: relámpago / en esta eternidad desnuda . . ." (in *Sombra del paraíso* [Buenos Aires: Editorial Losada, 1967], 73); or "El sol" (74).

15. André Breton, *Clair de terre,* 181.

16. Cernuda, *La realidad y el deseo,* 68.

17. Rubén Darío, *Azul* (Madrid: Espasa-Calpe, 1937), 144; Paz on Darío in *Cuadrivio* (Mexico City, 1967), 35.

18. Rimbaud, *Oeuvres,* 66–69; Baudelaire, *Les Fleurs du mal,* 57.

19. Alberto Valenzuela wrote of the book's "delirio y caos de ideas," in his "Nuevos ingenios mejicanos," *Abside* 22, no. 1 (January–March 1958):85.

20. Tomás Segovia, "Entre la gratuidad y el compromiso" and Manuel Durán, "La estética de Octavio Paz," *Revista mexicana de literatura* 8 (November–December 1956):102–13, 114–36.

21. H. Vendler, "Diary of the Poetic Process: *The Bow and the Lyre,*" *New York Times Book Review,* 30 June 1974, 23–24, 26. For an excellent introduction consult E. Rodríguez Monegal, "Relectura de *El arco y la lira,*" *Revista iberoamericana* 74 (January–February 1971):35–46.

22. André Breton, *Perspective cavalière* (Paris: Gallimard, 1970), 238–42.

23. M. Calvillo, "Poesía en alta voz," *Revista mexicana de literatura* 7 (September–October 1956):104–6. Consult R. Unger, *Poesía en voz alta in the Theater of Mexico* (Columbia: University of Missouri Press, 1981).

24. M. Rukeyser (1962), P. Miller (1963), S. Berg (1968–69), D. Gardner (1969), and L. Villaseñor (1970): all are noted in detail in the bibliography. See B. Péret, *Pierre de soleil* (Paris: Gallimard, 1962).

25. E. Carballo, "Octavio Paz," 3.

26. Ibid., 3.

27. Rimbaud, *Oeuvres,* 117.

28. Paz's lovely aphorism derives from Nietszche's "la vivacidad de la vida"—quoted by Paz (*A,* 155).

29. Rimbaud, *Oeuvres,* 104.

30. Pedro Salinas, *Poemas escogidos* (Buenos Aires: Editorial Losada, 1953), 62.

31. André Breton, *Manifestes*, 63; this echoes Rimbaud's: "La vraie vie est absente" (Rimbaud, *Oeuvres*, 103).

32. André Breton, *Arcane 17* (Paris: Gallimard, 1947), 83.

33. Pacheco, "Descripción," 183.

34. Ibid., 183.

35. E. Carballo, "Octavio Paz," 3.

36. L. Suárez, "Octavio Paz habla desde París," *México en la cultura* 560 (6 December 1959):2.

37. "Respuesta y algo más" (1960), 7.

38. José Luis Pacheco, "Nada se dice excepto lo indecible," *México en la cultura* 663 (26 November 1961):2.

39. Alejandra Pizarnik, "El premio internacional de poesía y *Salamandra*," *México en la cultura* 767 (1 December 1963):5.

40. Rubén Darío, *Prosas profanas*, 116: "¡Alabastros celestes habitados por astros: / Dios se refleja en esos dulces alabastros!"

41. "Absurdo y misterio," *Cuadernos americanos* 5, no. 5 (September–October 1942):239.

42. Pablo Neruda, *Residencia en la tierra* (Buenos Aires: Editorial Losada, 1958), 109–10.

43. André Breton, "Je demande l'occultation profonde, véritable du surréalisme" (1930), in *Manifestes*, 211. See Paz on this in *C*, 59–60, and *Pe*, 183.

44. Deleted from *Poemas* (1979); in *Salamandra* (Mexico City, 1962), 10.

45. André Breton, *Les pas perdus* (Paris: Gallimard, 1949), 171, often cited by Paz: *A*, 51, and *Conjunciones y disyunciones* (Mexico City, 1969), 22.

46. See Phillips, *Poetic Modes*, 109–13, on Paz's notion of transparency.

47. A. Lebrun, ed., *Lexique succint de l'érotisme* (Paris: Losfeld, 1970), 67.

48. *Poemas: Selección*, "Vox viva de México," no. 13 (Mexico City: U.N.A.M., 1961), recording.

49. Yves Bonnefoy, *Du mouvement et de l'immobilité de Douve* (Paris: Gallimard, 1970), 121, 104–9. See Wilson, *Octavio Paz*, 96–97.

50. Julio Cortázar, *Final del juego* (Buenos Aires: Editorial Sudamericana, 1964).

51. María Luisa Mendoza, "Algunas preguntas a Octavio Paz," *El gallo ilustrado* 6 (5 August 1962):1.

Chapter Four

1. Laus, "Octavio Paz hoy: la crítica de la significación," *Diorama de la cultura*, 16 April 1967, 1.

2. Stéphane Mallarmé, *Oeuvres complètes* (Paris: Gallimard, 1945), 366.

3. Lautréamont (I. Ducasse): "La poésie doit être faite par tous. Non par un" (in *Oeuvres complètes* [Paris: Gallimard, 1973], 311): quoted by Breton, *Manifestes*, 314.

4. *Los signos en rotación* (Buenos Aires: Sur, 1965), 19; hereafter cited in the text as *Si*.

5. Mallarmé: "The white spaces indeed become most important and strike first" (*Oeuvres*, 455).

6. Ibid., 456.

7. Cited by R. Gibson, *Modern French Poets on Poetry* (Cambridge: Cambridge University Press, 1961), 84.

8. Mallarmé, *Oeuvres*, 370.

9. Ibid., 38.

10. See Paz on André Breton's "magnetism" (in *C*, 57, 63).

11. Gibson, *Modern French Poets*, 88.

12. See Wilson, *Octavio Paz*, 139–40.

13. Gibson, *Modern French Poets*, 84.

14. Ibid., 79.

15. Ibid., 83.

16. *Claude Lévi-Strauss o el nuevo festín de Esopo* (Mexico City, 1967), 70; hereafter cited in the text as *Cl*.

17. Edmund Leach, "A Mexican Virgil and the Modern Inferno," *Listener* 87, no. 2238 (17 February 1972):218.

18. *Conjunciones y disyunciones* (Mexico City, 1969), 17; hereafter cited in the text as *Co*.

19. See N. O. Brown, *Life against Death: The Psychoanalytical Meaning of History* (New York: Random House, 1959), and *Love's Body* (New York: Random House, 1965).

20. See Juan Goytisolo, "El lenguaje del cuerpo," in *Octavio Paz*, ed. A. Roggiano, 293–305.

21. For an analysis of this poem see E. Caracciolo Trejo "Ustica," in *Aproximaciones*, ed. A. Flores, 187–88.

22. Breton, *Le surréalisme et la peinture*, 1.

23. This echoes Rimbaud: "Elle est retrouvée. / Quoi?—L'Eternité. / C'est la mer allée / Avec le soleil" (*Oeuvres*, 79).

24. For an analysis of this poem see Roberta Seabrook, "Vrindaban," in *Aproximaciones*, ed. A. Flores, 189–99.

25. See Julio Ortega, "Viento entero: el tiempo en un día," and Octavio Armand, "Viento entero," in *Aproximaciones*, ed. A. Flores, 200–208, 209–27.

26. Carlos Fuentes, "Mexico and its Demons," *New York Review of*

Books 20, no. 4 (20 September 1973):16; and *Posdata* (Mexico City, 1970), 95; hereafter cited in the text as *Pos.*

27. For further details see Paz's interview with Julio Scherer in *O*, 322–38, and Enrique Krauze, "Una lectura de *Tiempo nublado*," *Vuelta* 90 (May 1984):24–32.

28. In his magazine *Plural* 11 (August 1972):11–14.

29. In *Revista de la universidad de México* 32, no. 10 (June 1968):i–viii.

30. For more detailed analyses see Saul Yurkievich, "Topoemas," in *Aproximaciones*, ed. A. Flores, 254–58, and Rachel Phillips, "Topoemas: la paradoja suspendida," in *Octavio Paz*, ed. A. Roggiano, 221–28.

31. Jacques Roubaud in *Renga* (Paris: Gallimard, 1971), 36.

32. Published in *Libre* 1 (September–December 1971):64–66.

33. André Breton, *Les vases communicants* (Paris: Gallimard, 1955), 133.

34. For further readings of this text see Pere Gimferrer, "Convergencias," in *Octavio Paz*, ed. A. Roggiano, 307–16, and J. Alazraki, "*The Monkey Grammarian* or Poetry as Reconciliation," *World Literature Today* 56, no. 4 (Autumn 1982).

35. *Children of the Mire: Poetry from Romanticism to the Avant-Garde* (Cambridge: Harvard University Press, 1974), 44.

36. Memory is seen as a balcony in Baudelaire's "Le balcon" (in *Les Fleurs du Mal*, 38–39).

37. Rimbaud, *Oeuvres*, 69.

38. Bonnefoy, *Du mouvement*, 152.

39. For further readings of this poem see Juan Liscano, "Lectura libre de un libro de poesía de Octavio Paz," in *Octavio Paz*, ed. A. Roggiano, 347–61, and José Miguel Oviedo, "Los pasos de la memoria: Lectura de un poema de Octavio Paz," *Revista de Occidente* 14 (December 1976):42–51.

40. See Wilson, *Octavio Paz*, 166–75.

41. Vicente Huidobro's word play with "paracaídas/parasubidas" in *Altazor* (*Obras completas* [Santiago de Chile: Zig-Zag, 1964], 368)—noted by Andrés Sánchez Robayna, "Regreso y fundación," in *Octavio Paz*, ed. A. Roggiano, 367.

42. For more details see A. M. R. Rambo, "The Presence of Woman in the Poetry of Octavio Paz," *Hispania* 51, no. 2 (May 1968):259–64, and Wilson, *Octavio Paz*, 106–10.

43. X. Gauthier, *Surréalisme et sexualité* (Paris: Gallimard, 1968), 140.

44. Ibid., 275.

45. Breton, *Arcane 17*, 87–92, 44, 96, 98, 70.

46. Antonio Machado, *Obras: Poesía y prosa* (Buenos Aires: Editorial Losada, 1964), 320–23.

47. *Sor Juana Inés de la Cruz o las trampas de la fe* (Mexico City, 1982), 16; hereafter cited in the text as *So.*

48. Published in *Equivalencias* 1 (Winter 1980):8–13.

49. Published in *Vuelta* 8, 95 (October 1984):4.

Selected Bibliography

PRIMARY SOURCES

1. Poetry

Luna silvestre. Mexico City: Fábula, 1933.
Raíz del hombre. Mexico City: Simbad, 1937.
Bajo tu clara sombra y otros poemas sobre España. Valencia: Ediciones Españolas, 1937.
Entre la piedra y la flor. Mexico City: Nueva voz, 1941.
A la orilla del mundo y Primer día, Bajo tu clara sombra, Raíz del hombre, Noche de resurrecciones Mexico City: Compañía editora y Librera ARS, 1942.
Libertad bajo palabra. Mexico City: Tezontle, 1949.
¿Aguila o sol? Mexico City: Tezontle, 1951.
Semillas para un himno. Mexico City: Tezontle, 1954.
Piedra de sol. Mexico City: Tezontle, 1957.
La estación violenta. Mexico City: Fondo de cultura económica, 1958.
Libertad bajo palabra: obra poética (1935–1957). Mexico: Fondo de cultura económica, 1960. 2d ed., rev., 1968.
Salamandra (1958–1961). Mexico City: Joaquín Mortiz, 1962.
Blanco. Mexico City: Joaquín Mortiz, 1967.
Ladera este (1962–1968). Mexico City: Joaquín Mortiz, 1969.
La centena (Poemas: 1935–1968). Barcelona: Barral Editores, 1969.
Renga. Mexico City: Joaquín Mortiz, 1972.
El mono gramático. Barcelona: Editorial Seix-Barral, 1974.
Pasado en claro. Mexico City: Fondo de cultura económica, 1975.
Vuelta. Barcelona: Seix Barral, 1976.
Poemas (1935–1975). Barcelona: Seix Barral, 1979.

2. Prose

El laberinto de la soledad. Mexico City: Cuadernos americanos, 1950. 2d ed., rev. Mexico City: Fondo de cultura económica, 1959.
El arco y la lira; El poema; La revelación poética; Poesía e historia. Mexico City: Fondo de cultura económica, 1956.
Las peras del olmo. Mexico City: U.N.A.M., 1957.
Cuadrivio. Mexico City: Joaquín Mortiz, 1965.
Los signos en rotación, Buenos Aires: Sur, 1965.

Puertas al campo. Mexico City: U.N.A.M., 1966.
Claude Lévi-Strauss o el nuevo festín de Esopo. Mexico City: Joaquín Mortiz, 1967.
Corriente alterna. Mexico City: Siglo Veintiuno editores, 1967.
Marcel Duchamp o el castillo de la pureza. Mexico City: Era, 1968.
Conjunciones y disyunciones. Mexico City: Joaquín Mortiz, 1969.
Posdata. Mexico City: Siglo Veintiuno editores, 1970.
El signo y el garabato. Mexico City: Joaquín Mortiz, 1973.
Los hijos del limo: del romanticismo a la vanguardia. Barcelona: Seix Barral, 1974.
Xavier Villaurrutia en persona y en obra. Mexico City: Fondo de cultura económica, 1978.
El ogro filantrópico: historia y política 1971–1978. Mexico City: Joaquín Mortiz, 1979.
In/mediaciones. Barcelona: Seix Barral, 1979.
Sor Juana Inés de la Cruz o las trampas de la fe. Mexico City: Fondo de cultura económica, 1982.
Sombras de obras: Arte y literatura. Barcelona: Seix Barral, 1983.
Tiempo nublado. Barcelona: Seix Barral, 1983.
Hombres en su siglo y otros ensayos. Barcelona: Seix Barral, 1984.
Pasión crítica. Edited by H. Verani. Barcelona: Seix Barral, 1985. Interviews with Paz by Guibert, Ríos, Scherer, Fell, and others.

3. Translations

The Labyrinth of Solitude: Life and Thought in Mexico. Translated by Lysander Kemp. New York: Grove Press, 1961.
Sun Stone. Translated by Muriel Rukeyser. New York: New Directions, 1962.
Sun-Stone. Translated by Peter Miller. Toronto: Contact Press, 1963.
Selected Poems. Translated by Muriel Rukeyser. Bloomington: Indiana University Press, 1963.
"Altar of the Sun." Translated by Peter Berg. *Triquarterly* 13–14 (Winter 1968–69):167–84.
Piedra de sol: The Sun Stone. Translated by Donald Gardner. York: Cosmos Publications, 1969.
"Piedra de sol: Sun Stone." Translated by Laura Villaseñor. *Texas Quarterly* 3 (Autumn 1970):75–109.
Marcel Duchamp: Or the Castle of Purity. Translated by Donald Gardner. London: Cape Goliard Press, 1970.
Claude Lévi-Strauss: An Introduction. Translated by J. S. Bernstein and M. Bernstein. Ithaca: Cornell University Press, 1970.
¿Aguila o sol? Eagle or Sun? Translated by Eliot Weinberger. New York: October House, 1970. 2d ed. New York: New Directions, 1976.

Configurations. Translated by M. Rukeyser, Denise Levertov, Charles Tomlinson et al. New York: New Directions, 1971.

Renga: a Chain of Poems. Translated by Charles Tomlinson. New York: G. Brazilier, 1972.

The Other Mexico: Critique of the Pyramid. Translated by L. Kemp. New York: Grove Press, 1972.

Early Poems, 1935–1955. Translated by M. Rukeyser, Paul Blackburn, L. Kemp, D. Levertov, and W. C. Williams. New York: New Directions, 1973.

Alternating Current. Translated by Helen Lane. New York: Viking Press, 1973.

The Bow and the Lyre. Translated by Ruth L. Simms. Austin: University of Texas Press, 1973.

Children of the Mire: Poetry from Romanticism to the Avant-Garde. Translated by Rachel Phillips. Cambridge: Harvard University Press, 1974.

Conjunctions and Disjunctions. Translated by Helen Lane. New York: Viking Press, 1974.

The Siren and the Seashell and Other Essays on Poets and Poetry. Translated by L. Kemp and Margaret Sayers Peden. Austin: University of Texas Press, 1976.

A Draft of Shadows and Other Poems. Translated by E. Weinberger, Elizabeth Bishop, and Mark Strand. New York: New Directions, 1979.

Selected Poems. Edited by C. Tomlinson. Translated by C. Tomlinson, E. Bishop, E. Weinberger et al. Harmondsworth: Penguin Books, 1979.

The Monkey Grammarian. Translated by Helen Lane. New York: Seaver Books, 1981.

Airborn/Hijos del aire. London: Anvil Press, 1981. With C. Tomlinson.

Selected Poems. Edited by E. Weinberger. Translated by E. Weinberger, E. Bishop, L. Kemp et al. New York: New Directions, 1984.

One Earth, Four or Five Worlds: Reflections on Contemporary History. Translated by Helen Lane. New York: Harcourt Brace Jovanovich, 1985.

SECONDARY SOURCES

1. Bibliography
Verani, Hugo. *Octavio Paz: Bibliografía crítica.* Mexico City: U.N.A.M., 1983. An annotated critical bibliography essential for further study of the work and criticism of Paz.

2. Books and Parts of Books
Brotherston, Gordon. *Latin American Poetry: Origins and Presence.* Cambridge: Cambridge University Press, 1975. Chapter 7, "The Tradi-

tions of Octavio Paz," is a good overview, especially in relation to place and culture.

Céa, Claire. *Octavio Paz*. Paris: Editions Pierre Seghers, 1965. A useful introduction in French; photographs.

Flores, Angel, ed. *Aproximaciones a Octavio Paz*. Mexico City: Joaquín Mortiz, 1974. A collection of key essays on Paz's main themes and poems. See especially those by Juan García Ponce, Ramón Xirau, Jean Franco, Manuel Durán, Luis Mario Schneider, Carlos Magis, José Emilio Pacheco, Julio Ortega, Octavio Armand, and Enrique Pezzoni.

Gimferrer, Pere. *Lecturas de Octavio Paz*. Barcelona: Editorial Anagrama, 1980. An excellent close reading of Paz's main long poems *Piedra de sol, Blanco, Pasado en claro*, and "Nocturno de San Ildefonso" by one of Spain's best poets.

———, ed. *Octavio Paz*. Madrid: Taurus, 1982. A collection of essays on Paz with some overlap with A. Flores (1974) and A. Roggiano (1979).

Ivask, Ivar, ed. *The Perpetual Present: The Poetry and Prose of Octavio Paz*. Norman: University of Oklahoma Press, 1973. A collection of essays, with photographs. See essays by Emir Rodríguez Monegal, Allen W. Phillips, Manuel Durán, Ricardo Gullón, Tomás Segovia, and Ramón Xirau.

Magis, Carlos. *La poesía hermética de Octavio Paz*. Mexico City: El Colegio de Mexico, 1978. The first part is devoted to a close study of Paz's poetry up to the 1950s. The second is a thorough textual analysis of *La estación violenta*. Good on symbols.

Martínez Torrón, Diego. *Variables poéticas de Octavio Paz*. Madrid: Hiperion, 1979. A clear, readable, and thematic study of all Paz's work. It is informative and uses previous criticism well.

Phillips, Rachel. *The Poetic Modes of Octavio Paz*. Oxford: Oxford University Press, 1972. An excellent, concise study of Paz's work based on a division into four modes, the mythic, the surrealist, the semiotic, and modes in harmony.

Rodríguez Padrón, Jorge. *Octavio Paz*. Madrid: Jucar, 1975. A useful introduction with photographs and texts chosen by Paz.

Roggiano, Alfredo, ed. *Octavio Paz*. Madrid: Editorial Fundamentos, 1979. A collection of essays with some overlap with A. Flores (1974). See essays by Klaus Muller-Bergh, Judith Goetzinger, Thomas Mermall, Manuel Durán, and Juan Liscano.

Sucre, Guillermo. *La máscara, la transparencia: Ensayos sobre poesía hispanoamericana*. Caracas: Monte Avila, 1975. His "Octavio Paz: la vivacidad, la transparencia" and "El cuerpo del poema" are two of the most acute essays on Paz.

Wilson, Jason. *Octavio Paz: A Study of his Poetics*. Cambridge: Cambridge

University Press, 1979. This study explores Paz's affinities with André Breton's surrealism as the heretical basis to Paz's own vision of the poet and poem.

World Literature Today 56, no. 4 (Autumn 1982). A collection of essays honoring Paz for winning the Neustadt Prize. See those by Manuel Durán, Jaime Alazraki, José Miguel Oviedo, Hugo Verani, Julio Ortega, Juan Gustavo Cobo Borda, and Frances Chiles.

Xirau, Ramón. *Octavio Paz: el sentido de la palabra.* Mexico City: Joaquín Mortiz, 1970. A lucid and sympathetic account of Paz's work.

Yurkievich, Saul. *Fundadores de la nueva poesía latinoamericana: Vallejo, Huidobro, Borges, Girondo, Neruda, Paz.* Barcelona: Barral Editores, 1973. A succinct account of Paz's language and the avant-garde.

3. Articles

Alazraki, Jaime. "Para una poética del silencio." *Cuadernos hispanoamericanos* 343–45 (January–March 1979):157–84. A concise study of language and silence in Paz.

Benavides, Manuel. "Claves filosóficas de Octavio Paz." *Cuadernos hispanoamericanos* 343–45 (January–March 1979):11–42. A study of some of Paz's main preoccupations.

Bernard, Judith. "Myth and Structure in Octavio Paz's *Piedra de sol.*" *Symposium* 21, no. 1 (Spring 1967):5–13. A mythic, Jungian approach to Paz's major poem.

Fein, John. "The Mirror as Image and Theme in the Poetry of Octavio Paz." *Symposium* 10, no. 2 (Fall 1956):251–70. An early thematic study of an important image in Paz's poetry.

García Canclini, Nestor. "La poesía de Octavio Paz: de la palabra a la escritura." *Caravelle* 21 (1973):89–103. A subtle account leading to an analysis of *Blanco.*

King, Lloyd. "Surrealism and the Sacred in the Aesthetic Credo of Octavio Paz." *Hispanic Review* 37 (July 1969):382–93. A good exposition of Paz's surrealism at the level of ideas.

Mermall, Thomas. "Octavio Paz: *El laberinto de la soledad* y el sicoanálisis de la historia." *Cuadernos americanos* 27, 1 (January–February 1968):97–114. Excellent study of Paz's attitudes to history.

Nugent, Robert. "Structure and Meaning in Octavio Paz's *Piedra de sol.*" *Kentucky Foreign Language Quarterly* 13, no. 3 (1966):138–46. A concise account of Paz's key long poem.

Ortega, Julio. "Una hipótesis de lectura." *Revista de la universidad de México* 37, no. 8 (December 1981):41–44. A close reading of Paz's dense *Blanco.*

Oviedo, Miguel. "Los pasos de la memoria. Lectura de un poema de Octavio Paz." *Revista de Occidente* 14 (December 1976):42–51. Excellent reading of *Pasado en claro.*

Rodríguez Monegal, Emir. "Relectura de *El arco y la lira.*" *Revista iberoamericana* 74 (January–February 1971):35–46. A comparison of the first and second editions and Paz's debts to surrealism and existentialism.

Rodríguez Padrón, Jorge. "El tiempo hecho cuerpo repartido (Un análisis de 'Nocturno de San Ildefonso')." *Cuadernos hispanoamericanos* 343–45 (January–March 1979):591–614. A fine analysis of Paz's "Nocturno."

Segovia, Tomás. "Entre la gratuidad y el compromiso." *Revista mexicana de literatura* 8 (November–December 1956):102–13. An in-depth review of Paz's *El arco y la lira* in the year of its publication.

Wilson, Jason. "*Abrir/cerrar los ojos:* A Recurrent Theme in the Poetry of Octavio Paz." *Bulletin of Hispanic Studies* 48, no. 1 (January 1971):44–56. An analysis of a linguistic device that leads to Paz's debts to surrealism.

Index

161

DATE DUE

GAYLORD			PRINTED IN U.S.A.